Second Edition

Badminton

STEPS TO SUCCESS

Tony Grice

Human Kinetics

Library of Congress Cataloging-in-Publication Data

Grice, Tony.
  Badminton : steps to success / Tony Grice. -- 2nd ed.
    p. cm.
  ISBN-13: 978-0-7360-7229-8 (soft cover)
  ISBN-10: 0-7360-7229-2 (soft cover)
  1. Badminton (Game) I. Title.
  GV1007.G72 2008
  796.345--dc22

                    2007032476

ISBN-10: 0-7360-7229-2
ISBN-13: 978-0-7360-7229-8

The Web addresses cited in this text were current as of November 2007, unless otherwise noted.

Acquisitions Editor: Laurel Plotzke; **Developmental Editor:** Cynthia McEntire; **Assistant Editor:** Scott Hawkins; **Copyeditor:** Laura Brown; **Proofreader:** Kathy Bennett; **Graphic Designer:** Nancy Rasmus; **Graphic Artist:** Tara Welsch; **Cover Designer:** Keith Blomberg; **Photographer (cover):** Harry How/Getty Images; **Photographers (interior):** Dennis Fagan, Neil Bernstein; **Photo Asset Manager:** Laura Fitch; **Visual Production Assistant:** Joyce Brumfield; **Photo Office Assistant:** Jason Allen; **Art Manager:** Kelly Hendren; **Associate Art Manager:** Alan L. Wilborn; **Illustrator:** Alan L. Wilborn; **Printer:** Sheridan Books

We thank Louisiana State University in Shreveport, Louisiana, for assistance in providing the location for the photo shoot for this book.

Human Kinetics books are available at special discounts for bulk purchase. Special editions or book excerpts can also be created to specification. For details, contact the Special Sales Manager at Human Kinetics.

Printed in the United States of America   10 9 8 7 6 5 4 3 2

Human Kinetics
Web site: www.HumanKinetics.com

United States: Human Kinetics
P.O. Box 5076
Champaign, IL 61825-5076
800-747-4457
e-mail: humank@hkusa.com

Canada: Human Kinetics
475 Devonshire Road, Unit 100
Windsor, ON N8Y 2L5
800-465-7301 (in Canada only)
e-mail: info@hkcanada.com

Europe: Human Kinetics
107 Bradford Road
Stanningley
Leeds LS28 6AT, United Kingdom
+44 (0)113 255 5665
e-mail: hk@hkeurope.com

Australia: Human Kinetics
57A Price Avenue
Lower Mitcham, South Australia 5062
08 8372 0999
e-mail: info@hkaustralia.com

New Zealand: Human Kinetics
Division of Sports Distributors NZ Ltd.
P.O. Box 300 226 Albany
North Shore City, Auckland
0064 9 448 1207
e-mail: info@humankinetics.co.nz

Second Edition

Badminton

STEPS TO SUCCESS

◪ Contents

◫ Climbing the Steps to Badminton Success

I wrote this book to accomplish several goals. First, it has given me the opportunity to describe, demonstrate, and analyze my style of teaching and playing badminton. It is a book for players at all skill levels; for classes offered in high schools, colleges, clubs, and recreational programs; and for people who are learning to play on their own. It is a step-by-step process designed as a manual to teach you the game of badminton.

This is also a book for people who have played some badminton before. *Badminton: Steps to Success, Second Edition,* will help you examine your game and make corrections where you need them. The emphasis on fundamentals and strategy will allow you to analyze what you are doing on the badminton court. This book will be helpful in learning new skills, evaluating old skills, and improving what you are already doing.

If you want to reach the next level, you must read, ask questions, observe, imitate more experienced players, and most of all, practice and play badminton. *Badminton: Steps to Success, Second Edition,* provides the recipe for success. The only other elements you need to add are your talent, desire, and personality. I hope this step-by-step process helps you accomplish your goals and have fun as well.

The 11 steps in this book allow you to move from basic skills into game-like situations. There are more than 100 drills in this book to help you improve your skill, practice effectively, and record your progress. Suggested ways to increase or decrease the difficulty of the drills let you self-pace your progress to match your ability level. Missteps identify typical problems experienced by players learning badminton and provide suggestions for correcting those problems. You can apply the suggestions either during practice or during a game.

The 11 steps follow a learning sequence that I have developed over a long playing and teaching career. Each step prepares you for the next one and moves you closer to becoming the best badminton player you can be. Racket-handling skills and footwork precede learning to serve and are followed by the forehand and backhand overhead strokes. These basic skills are the foundation for more sophisticated strokes, such as the clear and drop shots; the smash; the drive; and more advanced overhead strokes, such as the around-the-head stroke. Step 9, a new chapter on scoring strategies, discusses the first major change in the rules for badminton in over 150 years. Steps 10 and 11 focus on success in doubles play and conditioning, respectively.

I hope this book will promote the sport of badminton to new heights around the world. Badminton is a wonderful game for all ages, truly a lifetime sport. It is great exercise and fun to play. As an Olympic sport as well as an extremely popular sport worldwide, badminton has a tremendous future.

Get ready to climb a staircase—one that will lead you to become a more skillful badminton player. You cannot leap to the top; you get there by climbing one step at a time. Each of the 11 steps you will take is an easy transition from the one before. The first few steps of the staircase provide a foundation—an understanding of the fundamental skills and techniques. As you progress, you will learn the elements you need in order to experience success on the badminton court. You will learn to combine the proper stroke production with game tactics during play to begin to make instinctive and accurate decisions in game situations. As you near the top of the staircase, your climb will become easier, and you'll find that you have developed confidence in your badminton abilities that will ensure further improvement and make playing the game more enjoyable.

To prepare to become a good climber, familiarize yourself with this section and The Sport of Badminton section for an orientation and to understand how to set up your practice sessions around the steps.

Follow the same sequence each step of the way:

1. Read the explanation of what the step covers, why the step is important, and how to execute or perform the step's focus, which may be a basic skill, concept, tactic, or combination of the three.

2. Study the figures to learn exactly how to position your body to execute each basic skill successfully.

3. Review the missteps, which note common errors and corrections.

4. Perform the drills. Drills help improve skills through repetition and purposeful practice. Read the directions and record your score. Drills are arranged in an easy-to-difficult progression. This sequence is designed to help you achieve continual success. Pace yourself by adjusting the drills to either decrease or increase the difficulty, depending on which best fits your ability. Drills appear near the skill instruction so you can refer to the instructions easily if you have trouble with the drill.

At the end of each step, have a qualified observer, such as a teacher, coach, or trained partner, evaluate your basic skill technique. This qualitative evaluation of your basic technique, or form, is vital because using correct form can enhance your performance.

You are now ready to begin your step-by-step journey to developing your badminton skills, building confidence, experiencing success, and having fun.

◨ Acknowledgments

I want to thank Human Kinetics for the opportunity to share my badminton experiences with others. I particularly want to thank two ladies—Elma Roane and Virginia Anderson of Memphis, Tennessee—for all the lessons they taught me. They were instrumental in introducing the game of badminton to me when I attended Memphis State University.

Dr. Charles "Red" Thomas and Northwestern State University of Louisiana also provided support for me in badminton as well as unique opportunities to learn. I am also grateful to Louisiana State University in Shreveport for its continued assistance and support. I also thank the United States Badminton Association for its cooperation and promotion of badminton.

A special thanks to Bob Roadcap for his friendship and interest in badminton. Also, I particularly wish to thank three colleagues who contributed to the second edition of this book by providing their thoughts, ideas, and drills. Soohyun Bang, the 1996 Olympic gold medalist in women's singles from South Korea, provided several drills and suggestions, especially in reference to singles play. Dr. Curt Dommeyer of Hermosa Beach, California, and California State University at Northridge provided valuable insight and comments relative to how the new rally scoring rules will affect strategy during badminton competition. Mike Gamez, a member of the USA Badminton board of directors and president of the Southern Badminton Association, offered his thoughts about advanced techniques and coaching. He also has a keen interest in promoting badminton at the junior level, especially in the southern United States.

I wish to thank the models who gave their time and talents to participate in the photo shoot: Soohyun Bang, Daniel Haston, Murthy Kotike, Jason Gills, Ty Moreno, and Cheryl Crain.

I would like to dedicate this new edition of *Badminton: Steps to Success* to my four children: Tony, Jr., David, Casey, and Curtis. And finally, I wish to express special appreciation to my sister and her husband, Ginger and Johnny Berryhill, for their love and support.

◫ The Sport of Badminton

Badminton is one of the most popular sports in the world. It appeals to all age groups and various skill levels, and men and women may play it indoors or outdoors for recreation as well as competition. The shuttlecock does not bounce and must be played in the air, thus making a fast game requiring quick reflexes and some degree of fitness. The badminton participant may also learn and appreciate the benefits of playing badminton socially, recreationally, and psychologically.

Badminton is a sport played over a net using rackets and shuttles with stroking techniques that vary from relatively slow to quick and deceptive movements. Indeed, shots during a rally may vary from extremes of 1 mile per hour on a drop shot to over 200 miles per hour on a smash. When played by experts, badminton is considered to be the fastest court game in the world. In the 2007 All-England Open Men's Doubles Final, one rally consisted of 92 shots, but lasted only one minute and eight seconds. A shot passed over the net every three-quarters of a second. However, both singles and doubles play may be controlled to meet individual needs and abilities for physical activity throughout your life.

BADMINTON HISTORY

Several games were forerunners of modern badminton, but the game's exact origin is unknown. Records describe a game with wooden paddles and a shuttlecock being played in ancient China, on the royal court of England in the twelfth century, in Poland in the early eighteenth century, and in India later in the nineteenth century. A game called *battledore and shuttlecock* involved hitting a shuttlecock with a wooden paddle known as a bat or *batedor* and was played in Europe between the eleventh and fourteenth centuries. The participants were required to keep the shuttle in play as long as possible.

Battledore and shuttlecock was played in a great hall called Badminton House in Gloucestershire, England, during the 1860s, and the name badminton was soon substituted for battledore and shuttlecock. The playing area of the hall was an hourglass shape, narrower in the middle than at the two ends. This suggested the need for playing the shuttle at a minimum height to keep the rally going. Badminton was played on this odd-shaped court until 1901. A string was added across the middle of the hall to make a rudimentary net. The original rules for badminton were standardized in 1887 and later revised in both 1895 and 1905. These rules still govern the sport today with the rally scoring system, effective January 2007, constituting a major change.

BADMINTON TODAY

Today, the Badminton World Federation (BWF) governs the game of badminton worldwide. The BWF, originally the International Badminton Federation (IBF), was founded in 1934 with nine member nations. In January 2007, the IBF adopted its new name, Badminton World

Federation. The BWF has grown to over 156 member nations and claims over 50 million members.

The Thomas Cup for men and the Uber Cup for women are the most prestigious world badminton competitions and are held in conjunction with each other. Both are organized on a two-year cycle in the even years. Players compete for the World Individual Championships in the odd-numbered years and for the Thomas Cup and the Uber Cup Championships in the even-numbered years. The World Mixed Doubles Championship, or Sudirman Cup, began in Jakarta, Indonesia, in 1989, and it coincides with the World Individual Championships. The major tournaments of the world make up the World Super Series. Players win points by competing in each tournament, and those accumulating the most points are invited to compete in the World Super Series Finals at the end of the year.

Badminton has been relatively unknown and unappreciated in the United States. Following its introduction in New York in 1878, the sport developed slowly. The American Badminton Association (ABA), the first national badminton organization in the United States, was formed in 1936. The ABA held the first U.S. National Championships in Chicago in 1937 and the first national junior tournament in 1947. The U.S. men's team played very well throughout the 1950s, making the final round of the Thomas Cup several times. The U.S. women dominated Uber Cup competition from 1957 through 1966. The first national intercollegiate championship was held in 1970. Interest and money in professional sports increased geometrically during the 1970s, but the general public's perception of badminton as a slow-paced, leisurely game was and is a misconception.

In recent years, interest has increased substantially. The ABA was reorganized in 1977 and became the United States Badminton Association (USBA). Badminton became a full medal sport for the 1992 Olympic Games in Barcelona, Spain. Badminton was a demonstration sport in the 1988 Olympics in Seoul, Korea. The inclusion of badminton as an Olympic sport encourages optimism for its future popularity, recognition, and success. In 1997, the USBA changed it's name to USA Badminton (USAB) primarily for marketing purposes. USA Badminton is currently the national governing body representing badminton on the United States Olympic Committee.

Currently, the best players in the world come from China, Europe, Korea, Malaysia, and Indonesia. However, U.S. players Tony Gunawan and Howard Bach won the men's doubles gold medal at the 2005 World Championships in Anaheim, California, becoming the first ever world men's doubles champions from the United States. In a 1993 study, it was reported that 300,000 people play badminton regularly in the United States and 760,000 call badminton their favorite sport. Badminton is currently the number-one sport in Great Britain, with almost two million registered badminton players. The Republic of China claims to have over 10 million badminton players. The BWF increased to 156 member nations in January 2007. In 2007, prize money for the World Super Series and final will exceed three million dollars. The future for both competitive and recreational badminton seems very bright.

COURT DIMENSIONS AND MARKINGS

The badminton court for singles play is 44 feet long (13.4 m) and 17 feet wide (5.2 m) (figure 1). The court for doubles play is 44 feet long and 20 feet wide (6.1 m). The net should be 5 feet and 1 inch (1.5 m) at the net poles, sloping to 5 feet at the top in the center of the net.

There is no official or standardized surface for badminton courts. A court may be indoors or outdoors; it may be concrete, asphalt, clay, grass, synthetic, or wood. However, most competitive badminton is played indoors, and because of the existing hardwood floors available in most university and school gymnasiums, wood is the most often used surface.

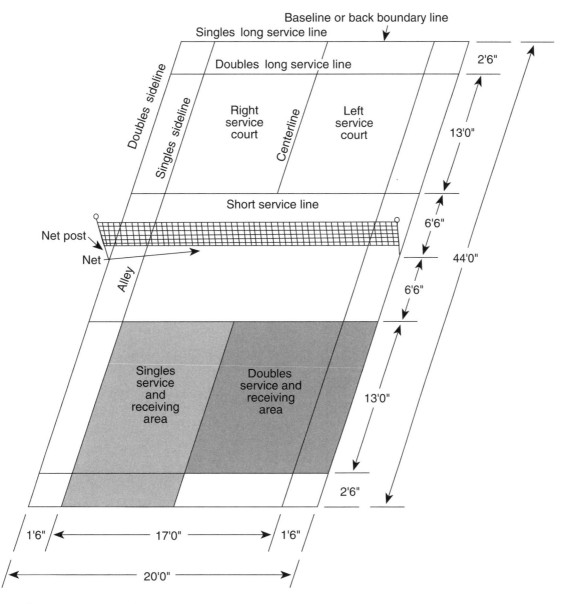

Figure 1 Court lines, areas, and dimensions.

EQUIPMENT AND GEAR

The cost and quality of what you wear, what you play with, and where you play varies greatly. Shorts, shirt, tennis shoes, or court shoes and socks are recommended, with a warm-up suit in cooler weather. White reflects heat better than darker colors and is cooler. Many players wear nylon, cycling shorts, or a cotton pant liner under their shorts for support and comfort. In addition, headbands, wristbands, and towels help keep perspiration from the face, eyes, and hands. A soft, leather glove is often used to provide a better grip and also to cushion the hand.

Newer, lighter rackets of boron, carbon, or graphite are often one piece in design and can be made of varying degrees of stiffness. There are also wide-body and oversize rackets for less air resistance and less torque. Strings are usually nylon or synthetic gut. Grip size is a personal preference. In the correct handshake grip, the thumb of the racket hand should touch the first knuckle of the middle finger.

A good medium-priced racket is suggested at first. It is a good idea to try hitting with several types of rackets before buying one. If possible, borrow one from a friend. Some stores have demonstration models that they will allow you to sample. Compare and choose the racket that feels the most comfortable to you.

The shuttle may be made from natural or synthetic materials. Nylon and feathered shuttles come in designated speeds. The speed of nylon shuttles are usually designated by the color of the band around the head of the shuttle. Red indicates fast, blue is medium, and green is slow. Physical education classes mainly use the nylon shuttle. The feathered shuttle is designed more for tournament play. The feathered shuttle must have 16 feathers attached to its base and must weigh between 4.74 and 5.50 grams. The weight of the feathered shuttle determines its speed. The lighter shuttle is designed for play in higher elevations, such as Mexico City. The heavier shuttle is for play in hotter, more humid climates nearer sea level. To test the speed of a shuttle, use a full underhand stroke, making contact over the back boundary line. A shuttle of correct speed should land not less than 1 foot, 9 inches (0.5 m) and not more than 3 feet, 3 inches (about 1 m) short of the opposite back boundary line on the opposite side of the net.

GAME RULES AND SCORE KEEPING

Decide who will serve first with a coin toss, a spin of the racket, or a toss and hit of the bird into the air to see toward who it points to when it lands. If you win the toss, you may choose to serve or receive or you can choose the side of the court you wish to start on. Whichever choice you make, your opponent gets to choose from the remaining options.

Both opponents begin the game by serving from the right court with zero or *love-all*. Anytime you are serving from the court in which you started, your score should be even. An illegal serve results in loss of serve and a point for your opponent.

Hit the serve diagonally across to your opponent. The feet of the server must be in the proper court and in contact with the floor until the serve is made. When the receiver is ready, the server has only one attempt to put the shuttle into play with an underhand (below the waist) serve. The receiver can stand anywhere in the proper court but must keep both feet in contact with the floor until the serve is delivered. The receiver is considered to have been ready if an attempt is made to hit the serve. After each rally or exchange, the server initiates the serve from the appropriate side depending on whether his or her score is odd or even. The score should always be announced before each service with the server's score given first. If a serve hits the top of the net and continues into the proper court, it is legal and play continues.

In both singles and doubles, the first serve is always made from the right side. This is because the server's score or serving team's score is zero, which is an even number. Anytime after the beginning of the game that the server's score or serving team's score is even (2, 4, 6, 8, and so on), the service is delivered from the right side. If a point is made and the score is odd (1, 3, 5, 7, and so on), the server serves from the left side. The server's score dictates which side he or she serves from.

In doubles, one partner starts on the right side and one partner starts on the left side. Where you start is your even court. If the score is odd, partners should be opposite of where they started. If a point is made, the server changes courts and serves diagonally across to the other side. Your score dictates which side you serve from after your opponents have lost their serve. If one partner loses her serve, it is called *service over* or *side out*. Your opponents now have the chance to serve. Just as in singles, all doubles games are played to 21 points.

In singles play, the service court is long and narrow. The side alley is out of bounds; the back alley is in bounds or good. The serve must carry past the short service line, which is 6.5 feet (about 2 m) from the net, and must not carry beyond the back boundary line. The lines are considered part of the court and in bounds. A bird that lands on a line is considered to be good. Read step 9 to learn the strategy involved in returning the singles serve and winning the singles rally.

The service court in doubles play is short and fat. The side alley is in bounds and the back alley is out of bounds on the serve. However, once the bird is in play, the back alley is good. The serve must carry past the short service line and must not carry beyond the doubles long service line. Step 10 explains strategies involved in returning the doubles serve and winning the doubles rally. Games normally are played to 21 points in all events.

During the early 1990s, the IBF experimented with a new scoring system for singles, doubles, and mixed doubles, in which games were played to nine points and the winner of the match was the player who won three out of five games. There was no setting or extension of a tied game as defined in the original rules. Also there was no requirement of winning by a minimum of two points. That attempt at changing the scoring was temporary and only slightly successful so the older method of keeping score was retained for the next decade. The WBF now supports the elimination of the older scoring method that included games to both 15 and 11 points along with the unique concept of setting. At its annual general membership meeting, the former IBF voted to adopt the rally point system for all IBF sanctioned events. The USAB Board of Directors voted to adopt this policy for all USAB national ranking tournaments. Nonranking tournaments that wish to be sanctioned by USAB would not be required to use rally scoring at this time. The rationale for this suggested change was to make the sport more marketable to spectators and television, as well as to improve the sport's acceptance and understanding by the general population. Preliminary observations indicate match time may be reduced by as much as 25 percent. The rally scoring system requires players to be more alert and to score quickly in these abbreviated games. Athletes will be required to adapt to a new strategy for winning matches, but they will also benefit from this exciting and potentially pressure-packed format.

The simplified new rally points scoring system as amended and adopted by the BWF and USAB effective August 2006 is summarized in the sidebar "Simplified New Rally Points Scoring System."

In summary, you win the rally and a point if your opponent

- fails to deliver a legal serve;
- fails in attempting to return a legal serve;
- hits the shuttle outside the proper boundary lines;
- hits the shuttle into the net;
- hits the shuttle two or more times on a return;
- touches the net with his or her body or racket while the shuttle is in play;
- lets the shuttle hit the floor inside the court;
- deliberately carries or catches the bird on the racket;
- does anything to hinder or interfere with your return;
- encroaches under the net with his or her feet, body, or racket;
- reaches over the net to hit a return;
- touches the bird with anything other than his or her racket; or
- fails to keep both feet in contact with the floor while serving or receiving.

Any point that has to be replayed is called a *let*. These should occur very rarely and are usually the result of some outside interference.

Simplified New Rally Points Scoring System

Scoring System

- A match consists of the best of three games, each game played to 21 points.
- The side winning a rally adds a point to its score.
- At 20-all, the side that gains a 2-point lead first wins the game.
- At 29-all, the side scoring the 30th point wins the game.
- The side winning a game serves first in the next game.

Intervals and Change of Ends

- When the leading score reaches 11 points, players have a 60-second interval in order to change ends of the court.
- A 2-minute rest interval between each game is allowed.
- In the third game, players change ends when either side scores 11 points.

Singles Scoring

- At the beginning of the game and when the server's score is even, the server serves from the right service court. When the server's score is odd, the server serves from the left service court.
- If the server wins a rally, the server scores a point and then serves from the alternate service court.
- If the receiver wins a rally, the receiver scores a point and becomes the new server. The new server serves from the right service court if his score is even or from the left service court if his score is odd.

Doubles Scoring

- There is only one service opportunity per side in doubles. Both partners no longer get a chance to serve. Your score dictates which partner will serve. When the serving team commits a fault, the service changes to the opposing team. Their score then determines which side the next serve will be delivered from.
- At the beginning of the game and when the server's score is even, the server serves from the right court. When the server's score is odd, the server serves from the left court.
- If the serving side wins a rally, the serving side scores a point and the same server serves again from the alternate service court.
- If the receiving side wins a rally, the receiving side scores a point. The receiving side becomes the new serving side.
- The player of the receiving side who served last stays in the same service court from where he or she last served.
- The players do not change their respective service courts until they win a point when their side is serving.
- If players commit an error in the service court, the error is corrected when the mistake is discovered.

WARM-UP AND COOL-DOWN

A good warm-up should prepare you for strenuous activity without tiring you out. A general warm-up to increase your blood circulation might begin with light calisthenics or jogging around the court. Combine running toward the net with backpedaling away from the net, along with shuffling sideways across the court while facing the net.

After you have warmed your muscles and increased your circulation, you are ready to stretch your upper body, shoulders, back, and legs. Move through a series of basic stretches slowly with little or no bouncing before playing. Research indicates passive or static stretching is better for you and less likely to cause injury. Hold each stretch for approximately 20 seconds.

Now you are ready to hit. Include about 5 to 10 minutes of easy hitting while practicing specific shots. Start in the midcourt with controlled, easy exchanges with your practice partner or opponent. Begin with overhead strokes on both the forehand and backhand sides to further warm-up and stretch your shoulders, upper body, and legs. Next, move laterally, reaching to hit returns from either side of your body. Move from the backcourt near the baseline toward the net, alternating returns with your partner to move each other from frontcourt to backcourt. Alternate roles with your partner to practice clears, drop shots, and smashes. Practice drop shots from backcourt, while your partner returns them with underhand clears from up at the net.

After strenuous activity, cool-down by allowing your body to gradually return to a normal pace. Walk the perimeter of the court for about 5 minutes or until your heart rate returns to around 100 beats per minute. Then repeat your stretching exercises. This cool-down helps to get rid of lactic acid built up during vigorous exercise and helps to prevent muscle soreness. Recent research indicates drinking sports drinks before, during, and after strenuous physical activity may also prevent muscle soreness. Dehydration is the primary cause of muscle cramps so an adequate amount of water should be consumed as well.

Badminton requires a certain level of fitness. In close matches, fitness usually is a factor in the outcome. Important considerations in your conditioning program are exercise, a sound diet, adequate sleep, rest, and practice. Step 11 discusses the need for the more advanced player to adopt a more rigorous and structured training program.

RESOURCES

This section lists additional resources you can use to find out more about badminton. Organizations such as the BWF and USA Badminton list tournament locations, state organizations, and local badminton clubs that have leagues and weekly recreational play. Both the BWF and USA Badminton have Web sites, e-mail addresses, and telephone numbers where they can be contacted:

USA Badminton
One Olympic Plaza
Colorado Springs, CO 80909
719-866-4808
usab@usabadminton.org
www.usabadminton.org

Badminton World Federation
Batu 3 1/2 Jalan Cheras
56000 Kuala Lumpur, Malaysia
Tel: +6-03-9283 7155
FAX: +6-03-9284 7155
bwf@internationalbadminton.org
www.internationalbadminton.org

◧ Key to Diagrams

------------>   path of player

——————→   path of shuttle (bird)

A, B, C, D   players

■   target area

1, 2, 3   order of hits

Racket Handling and Footwork

"Float like a butterfly, sting like a bee" is an often-quoted line from former heavyweight boxing champion Muhammad Ali. It is an excellent description of how you need to move and hit in badminton play. Good footwork entails reaching the bird as fast as possible with as little effort as possible, like the butterfly. It gets you into the best position to execute your shots, or sting like a bee, while maintaining good balance and body control.

This step will get your hands and feet ready to execute efficiently. The various ways to hold your racket for a forehand, backhand, serve, and other shots are discussed and illustrated later. Making racket handling and footwork a habit requires practice and repetition, along with some additional thought during play.

HANDLING THE RACKET

Getting accustomed to the feel and weight of the racket (figure 1.1) prepares you to handle it comfortably during play. You learn or sense how far away the racket is from your body. This is the beginning of your eye–hand–racket coordination, which is essential in making contact with the bird. Beginning players often swing and miss the bird completely. This sense of feel or timing plays a very important role in your stroke production. Beginners may hit the shuttle with the frame or make contact somewhere other than the center of the strings. Practice in hitting, blocking, bouncing, or even picking up the shuttle with your racket reinforces the way the racket feels and enhances your racket-handling skill. Try to improve your eye–hand coordination by creating your own racket-handling drill or use those suggested in this step.

Good badminton players constantly move the racket around in their hands. The light racket makes it possible to use wrist action initiated by forearm rotation, and therefore you can manipulate the racket at a greater speed. In addition to the lighter racket, the lightness of the shuttle makes possible greater use of the wrist without loss of control. Your racket head may be moving at a terrific speed as you throw it out to meet the shuttle. This indicates you need a firm grip at contact. However, it is essential not to grip your racket too tightly. Ideally, your grip in badminton

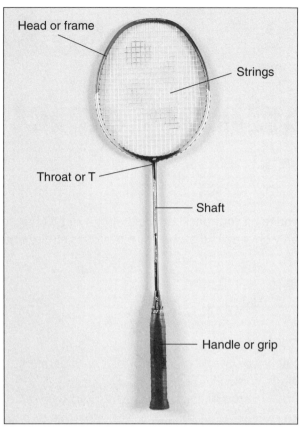

Figure 1.1 Parts of the racket.

should provide flexible and effortless movement of the wrist and a comfortable and secure grip with your dominant hand.

The forehand grip is sometimes referred to as either the pistol grip or the handshake grip (figure 1.2*a*). Slide the racket into your hand as if shaking hands with it. Your right forefinger is slightly apart from the other fingers, providing the trigger finger effect as in holding a pistol. If your racket is perpendicular to the floor, then you are holding the racket correctly. It is almost identical to the Eastern forehand grip in tennis. The advantage of the handshake grip is that it enables you to hit all shots without changing your grip.

| Figure 1.2 | **Handshake Grip** |

a

b

FOREHAND

1. Shake hands with your racket
2. Reach for the shuttle with arm extended
3. Snap your racket through with emphasis on forearm rotation

BACKHAND

1. Shake hands with your racket
2. Place your thumb straight up and down on top left-hand bevel

For the backhand, the only change is that your thumb is straight up and down on the top left-hand bevel of the handle instead of wrapped around it (figure 1.2b). The thumb-up grip provides added support and leverage for all backhand strokes. A slight rotation along with a change in finger pressure creates less stress for the elbow, wrist, and hand of the racket arm. This slight change also contributes to an increase in power and ease of movement in the backhand stroke when executed properly.

Misstep

You don't have enough time to change or adjust your grip for the backhand.

Correction

Use a handshake (pistol) grip, which allows you to hit your backhand with only a slight change from your forehand. For the backhand, the only change is that that your thumb is straight up and down on the top left-hand bevel of the handle instead of wrapped around it.

GETTING INTO READY POSITION

An alert, ready position enables you to move quickly as soon as you determine the direction of your opponent's return. In the ready position, your feet are square or staggered slightly with the dominant foot slightly forward of the nondominant foot. Your weight is on the balls of your feet, which are spread about shoulder-width apart with your knees slightly bent (figure 1.3). Hold the racket head up in front of your body and slightly on the backhand side. Hold your racket with a handshake, or pistol, grip.

Players vary this ready position to meet their own style and needs. Some players stagger their feet slightly to be ready to move to the side, to the net, or to the backcourt more quickly from the center court position. This is necessary when you are waiting to receive the serve because you must have your feet in a staggered or up-and-back position to anticipate a flick serve or drive serve. (See step 2 for more on serves.) In this waiting position, the dominant foot is back and the nondominant foot is forward. Your racket is usually held slightly higher in doubles play than it is when receiving in singles play. This higher position allows you to react more quickly to a flick, drive, or poor (higher than desirable)

Figure 1.3 Ready position.

short serve. After your long singles serve, you assume the ready position with your feet square or staggered slightly with the dominant foot approximately 6 inches (15 cm) forward of the nondominant foot.

Misstep

The bird gets behind you.

Correction

Keep your racket up and move quickly as soon as you determine the direction of your opponent's return.

Ready Position Drill. *Ready Position*

Assume the ready position, keeping your feet shoulder-width apart with your knees slightly bent and your weight on the balls of your feet. Check your partner's stance and ask her or him to check yours. Refer to figure 1.3, page 3. Complete five repetitions.

Success Check

- Hold your racket head up, slightly on your backhand side.
- Hold your nondominant arm up and slightly bent.

- Keep your feet about shoulder-width apart with your weight on the balls of your feet.

Score Your Success

Five perfect ready positions = 5 points

Three or four perfect ready positions = 3 points

One or two perfect ready positions = 1 point

Your score ____

MOVING YOUR FEET

You need to move your feet to hit the shuttle in badminton play. The focus of good footwork is reaching the bird as quickly as possible with as little effort as possible. Good footwork gets you into the best position to execute shots while maintaining good balance and body control. You can use each of the following footwork techniques to move on the badminton court.

Step-close step (figure 1.4). From the ready position, the nondominant foot is always the pivot foot and the dominant, or racket-hand foot, is the leading foot. Reaching for the shuttle with the dominant arm and leg saves time, and the subsequent push off or jump off of the dominant leg aids in a swift recovery. As you move forward or backward, you must pivot and move, reaching with the dominant leg as you also reach with your racket to intercept the shuttle. Diagonal movement to the front or back court is your goal. Lead with the dominant leg, taking a step-close step, shuffling, or sliding your feet in the desired

direction, either forehand or backhand. Recover to midcourt in a three-step sequence.

Shuffle step (figure 1.5). The shuffle step is executed primarily when moving forward toward the net or backward toward the non-dominant side. It is an optional approach used to move quickly to the backhand side of the backcourt. Reverse pivot and shuffle your feet with the dominant foot leading toward the rear backhand side of the court. Deliver an overhead forehand or around-the-head return. The hips and shoulders rotate quickly as you throw the racket up to meet the oncoming shuttle. The legs scissor with the dominant leg swinging forward. The nondominant leg swings backward, absorbing most of the body's weight on landing and propelling you back toward centercourt.

To move quickly to the net from the ready position, the nondominant leg swings forward at a diagonal either to the front right or the front left, depending on the desired direction. The domi-

a

b

c

Figure 1.4 Step-close step.

a

b

c

Figure 1.5 Shuffle step.

nant leg then lunges forward, crossing over and almost jumping in the direction of the dropping shuttle. This two-step maneuver propels you to the net in an explosive manner. The subsequent push-off of this dominant leg and foot propels you back to centercourt.

Sashay step (figure 1.6). From the ready position, your nondominant foot will be the pivot foot and the dominant, or racket-hand, foot will be the leading foot. Pivot and move forward or backward at a diagonal. Lead with the dominant

leg as before, but do not shuffle or use the step-close step. Instead, use a sashay step on your second step, moving your nondominant foot behind and beyond your front foot and in the direction that you are moving. This action allows you to move farther and faster to the net. Forehand and backhand returns require you to recover to midcourt using the same three-step pattern as before: racket leg, other leg, racket leg. From backcourt, the scissoring action of your legs helps to propel you back to centercourt.

a

b

c

Figure 1.6 Sashay step.

Three-step sequence to return to midcourt (figure 1.7). This action allows you to move farther and faster to the net. Forehand and backhand returns require you to recover to midcourt using the same three-step pattern as before: racket leg, other leg, racket leg. The scissoring action of your legs helps to propel you back to centercourt after your overhead returns from backcourt. The hips and shoulders rotate quickly as you throw the racket up to meet the oncoming shuttle. The legs scissor with the dominant leg swinging forward. The nondominant leg swings backward, absorbing most of the body's weight on landing and propelling you back toward centercourt. You then recover to midcourt using the same three-step pattern as before—racket leg, other leg, racket leg—and assume ready position.

a b c

Figure 1.7 Three-step return to midcourt.

Footwork Drill 1. *Shuffle-Slide-Shadow Footwork*

From the ready position, the nondominant foot is always the pivot foot and the dominant (racket-hand foot) is the leading one. Reaching for the shuttle with the dominant arm and leg saves time and the subsequent push-off of the dominant leg aids in a swift recovery. Pivot and move forward toward the net, reaching with the racket as if intercepting a shuttle dropping near the net. Alternate moving diagonally to the right front court and then the left front court. Practice changing from the forehand grip to the backhand grip. Lead with the dominant leg, taking a step-close step, shuffling, or sliding your feet in the desired direction, either forehand or backhand. Recover to midcourt in a three-step sequence.

Success Check

- Reach for the shuttle with your dominant arm and leg.
- Switch from a forehand to a backhand grip.
- Recover to midcourt.

Score Your Success

Perform the drill for 5 minutes = 5 points

Your score ___

Footwork Drill 2.   *Gravity Shadow Footwork*

If more speed is required or a greater distance is to be covered, a slight change allows gravity to assist you in starting or reversing your direction to and from the net. Instead of simply pivoting the non-dominant foot from the ready position, you move it slightly backward as you pivot in the opposite direction. This movement will cause you to fall in the desired direction with the aid of gravity. Normally, the subsequent push-off of the dominant leg aids in a swift recovery, but if you bring the nondominant foot forward as well then plant both feet and lean backward, the subsequent push-off from both feet greatly assists gravity in helping you change direction. Move forward toward the net at a diagonal, reaching with your racket arm, alternating from a forehand grip to a backhand grip. Fall in the desired direction, either forehand or backhand, and lead with the dominant leg, taking a step-close step. Reach with your racket as if to intercept a shuttle dropping close to the net, then bring the nondominant foot up and under to help you return to midcourt.

Success Check

- Switch from a forehand to a backhand grip as you move toward the net.
- Lead with your dominant leg as you take a step-close step.
- Return to midcourt.

Score Your Success

Perform the drill for 5 minutes = 5 points

Your score ___

Footwork Drill 3.   *Sashay Step Shadow Footwork*

Assume the ready position. In this drill, your nondominant foot will be the pivot foot and the dominant or racket-hand foot will be the leading one. Pivot and move forward toward the net at a diagonal. Alternate from a forehand grip to a backhand grip and simulate reaching for a shuttle dropping near the net. Lead with the dominant leg as before, but do not shuffle or use the step-close step. Instead, use a sashay step on your second step, moving your nondominant foot behind and beyond your front foot and closer to the net. This action allows you to move farther and faster to the net. Repeat the simulated forehand and backhand returns from the net and then recover to midcourt using the same three-step pattern as before: racket leg, other leg, racket leg.

Success Check

- Move toward the net at a diagonal.
- Switch from a forehand to a backhand grip.
- Lead with your dominant leg and take a sashay step.
- Recover to midcourt.

Score Your Success

Perform the drill for 5 minutes = 5 points

Your score ___

Footwork Drill 4. *Footwork and Movement*

Starting from centercourt and the ready position, touch the four corners of the court in succession, returning to the center position after each touch (figure 1.8). Pivot and reach with your dominant arm and leg, and shuffle using a step-close stepping action with your feet. Cross over only on your backhand side, not your forehand side. Perform the drill for 30 seconds.

To Increase Difficulty

- Perform the maximum number of touches that you can in 30 seconds.
- Simulate swinging at and hitting an imaginary bird at the end of each touch or reach.
- Without a racket in your hand, reach and touch the floor with your dominant hand.
- Use a sashay step instead of the normal step-close step shuffle.
- Pivot, step-close jump, and simulate a stroking action at the end. Return to center court.

This jumping action requires much more energy, and you should attempt to stay under control and on balance, especially landing from the jump.

To Decrease Difficulty

- Slow down. Walk or shuffle your feet more slowly.

Success Check

- Reach with your dominant hand.
- Lead with your dominant foot.

Score Your Success

Touch the four corners 20 times or more in 30 seconds = 5 points

Touch the four corners 15 to 19 times in 30 seconds = 3 points

Touch the four corners 10 to 14 times in 30 seconds = 1 point

Your score ___

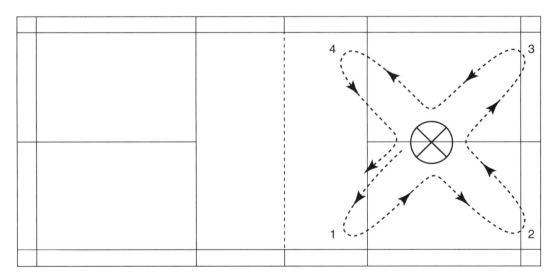

Figure 1.8 Footwork and movement drill.

GETTING READY FOR SHOTS

From the ready position, watch the bird leave your opponent's racket and expect the bird to come back over the net to your side of the court every time. Because the shuttle rarely comes to you during a rally, most shots are hit on the run. One way to get there is to take small, bouncy steps, shuffling or sliding into position to hit. You should try to recover to midcourt after every return. However, stop where you are before your opponent's return even if it is not possible to get completely back to centercourt. It is essential not to be moving when your opponent hits the shuttle. It will be easier to go farther from a standstill than change direction while moving.

As your opponent gets ready to hit, watch his or her racket. Focus on the bird, and wait until you are sure of the direction the shuttle is trav-eling before moving (figure 1.9a). Do not guess or anticipate too soon. From the ready position, as soon as you determine the direction of the return, pivot, reach with the dominant foot, shuffle or take a step-close step or skip. Keep your feet close to the floor and cross your feet over when you move to the backhand, but not the forehand side (figure 1.9b).

When you go to the net, your dominant leg is normally leading and pushes off to return to midcourt (figure 1.9c). However, if you also bring the nondominant foot forward and plant it near the dominant foot then lean backward, the subsequent push-off with both legs greatly assists in changing direction and propelling you back to centercourt even faster.

Figure 1.9   Ready Position and Footwork

PREPARATION

1. Place your feet shoulder-width apart
2. Keep your toes straight
3. Square your feet or stagger them slightly
4. Flex your knees
5. Place your weight on balls of your feet
6. Hold your racket up
7. Apply handshake (pistol) grip
8. Keep your eyes on the bird

a

EXECUTION

1. See the bird and your opponent
2. Pivot
3. Lead with your dominant foot and step-close step or shuffle your feet
4. Use crossover step only on backhand

b

FOLLOW-THROUGH

1. Reach with your dominant arm and leg
2. Push off your lead foot or both feet
3. After the shot, propel yourself back to midcourt
4. Repeat three-step pattern in reverse on backhand
5. Keep your balance

c

Misstep

Your dominant leg gets very tired from going up to the net.

Correction

Divide the workload evenly between the two legs by pulling the trailing leg up under the body and pushing back with both legs.

Lack of awareness or practice usually causes problems with racket handling, achieving the ready position, and movement on the court. Very few players emphasize this part of their game. Your racket should become an extension of your hand, with your grip comfortable and firm without any need to think about it. You should consistently recover or fall back to your centercourt position instinctively. Spend some time practicing and repeating drills to develop speed and efficient movement on the court.

Misstep

You experience inconsistent shots or rallies caused by failure to recover to your ready position.

Correction

Get in good shape so you can move quickly and effortlessly. Fatigue often causes inconsistency. Return quickly to centercourt after each shot and stop before your opponent hits his or her return. During your opponent's stroke, focus on the bird as long as possible. Try to see the shot hit your opponent's racket and don't focus on his or her upper-body movements.

Racket and Bird Control Drill 1. *Handshake*

Take turns with your partner shaking hands with the racket handle to learn the pistol grip. Start with the racket on edge. Grasp the racket handle as if you were shaking hands with it. Slide the racket into your hand with your forefinger slightly apart from your other fingers. This provides the trigger finger effect as if you were holding a pistol. As you shake hands, your racket should be lying across your palm and fingers with your thumb and index finger forming a V on top of your racket handle. It is almost identical to the Eastern forehand grip in tennis. Check your partner's grip and ask her or him to check yours. Complete five repetitions.

To Increase Difficulty

* Execute the pistol grip with your eyes closed. Have your partner or teacher check your grip for correct position.

* Change to the backhand grip by placing your thumb in a straight-up position on the top left-hand bevel of your racket handle.

Success Check

* Hold your racket perpendicular to floor, edge down.
* Form a V on top of your racket handle.
* Grasp your racket firmly.

Score Your Success

Five perfect handshake grips = 5 points

Three or four perfect handshake grips = 3 points

One or two perfect handshake grips = 1 point

Your score ___

Racket and Bird Control Drill 2. *Shuttle Bounce*

Use your pistol grip and bounce the shuttle off the face of your racket up in the air (figure 1.10). Bounce the bird vertically off both sides of the racket face. This teaches you to keep your eyes on the bird and helps you to get the feel of the bird contacting the racket face. Continue until you can successfully bounce the bird several times without missing. Attempt to complete 30 consecutive bounces with your palm up and 30 consecutive bounces with your palm down.

Figure 1.10 Shuttle bounce.

To Increase Difficulty

- Alternate hitting the shuttle with palm up and then palm down.
- Bump the bird 3 to 4 feet (about 1 m) in the air.

Success Check

- Bump the bird into the air with the strings of your racket.
- Lift your racket and allow the bird to travel only 1 to 2 feet (about 0.5 m) in the air.

Score Your Success

Complete 20 or more consecutive bounces with your palm up = 5 points

Complete 10 to 19 consecutive bounces with your palm up = 3 points

Complete 1 to 9 consecutive bounces with your palm up = 1 point

Your score ___

Complete 20 or more consecutive bounces with your palm down = 5 points

Complete 10 to 19 consecutive bounces with your palm down = 3 points

Complete 1 to 9 consecutive bounces with your palm down = 1 point

Your score ___

Your total score ___

Racket and Bird Control Drill 3. *Shuttle Scoop*

Use the handshake grip with your palm up. Pick or scoop up a bird lying on the floor, attempting to keep the bird on the racket face. Place your racket face next to the bird with the racket face held nearly parallel to the floor (figure 1.11). Slide the racket quickly under the bird with a scooping action, allowing the wrist to roll under and catching the bird on the racket face. Right-handed players usually do this from the right side of the bird. Complete five repetitions.

To Increase Difficulty

- Scoop up the shuttle and toss it into the air, catching it with your opposite hand.
- Scoop up the shuttle while holding the racket palm down or with a backhand grip.
- Scoop up the shuttle from both the right side and the left side.

To Decrease Difficulty

- Place the shuttle on the floor pointing directly upward, feathers down. A bird that is sitting up will more easily fall onto the racket face.

Success Check

- Bird remains on racket face.

Score Your Success

Successfully scoop up bird five times = 5 points

Successfully scoop up bird three or four times = 3 points

Successfully scoop up bird one or two times = 1 point

Your score ___

Figure 1.11 Shuttle scoop.

Racket and Bird Control Drill 4. *Shuttle Toss and Catch*

Hold your racket in a handshake grip with the palm up. Place the shuttle on the racket face. Lift the racket quickly and toss the shuttle 2 to 3 feet (0.6 to 1 m) in the air. As the shuttle drops, catch the shuttle on the open face of the racket with the racket hand palm up. By lowering the racket face under the dropping shuttle and subtly giving with the catch, you allow the shuttle to slow down gradually and not bounce off the face of the racket. Complete five tosses and catches.

Success Check

- Check your grip to make sure that you are using the proper handshake grip.
- Bird remains on the racket face.

Score Your Success

Five successful tosses and catches = 5 points

Three or four successful tosses and catches = 3 points

One or two successful tosses and catches = 1 point

Your score ___

Racket and Bird Control Drill 5. *Bird Carry*

From the ready position, use the pistol grip with your palm up. Place a bird on your racket strings and walk to the net from the back boundary line using a step-close step shuffle movement with your feet (figure 1.12). Lead with your dominant foot, keeping the shuttle on the racket. Hold your nondominant arm up for balance.

Figure 1.12 Bird carry.

To Increase Difficulty

- Shuffle or skip to the net from the back boundary line as fast as possible without letting the bird fall off your racket face.
- With the bird on your strings, compete with your partner in a race from the back boundary line to the net and back.
- Use the pistol grip, holding your hand palm down or in backhand position. Place the bird on the strings and shuffle to and from the net.

To Decrease Difficulty

- Go slower and walk from the back boundary line to the net and back.

Success Check

- Use a handshake (pistol) grip.
- Hold your palm up.
- Lead with your dominant foot.

Score Your Success

Complete one round trip to the net from the back boundary line without dropping the bird = 5 points

Complete one round trip to the net from the back boundary line, dropping the bird once = 3 points

Complete one round trip to the net from the back boundary line, dropping the bird twice = 1 point

Your score ___

SUCCESS SUMMARY OF RACKET HANDLING AND FOOTWORK

If you can handle your racket without thinking about it, assume your ready position, and readily move around your side of the court, you are well on your way to becoming a better badminton player. In badminton, the lighter racket makes it possible for you to use wrist action initiated by forearm rotation to manipulate the racket at a great speed. The lighter object (shuttle) also makes it possible for greater use of your wrist without loss of control. This indicates that you need a firm grip at the instant you make con-

tact. The handshake (pistol) grip in badminton provides flexible and effortless movement of your wrist when hitting the bird.

Movement on the badminton court is concerned with reaching the shuttle in as few steps as possible while maintaining good balance and keeping your body under control. With practice, proper footwork eventually becomes habit and virtually an automatic aspect of your game.

Before you advance to the next step, record and tally your drill scores from this step.

Ready Position Drill	
1. Ready Position	___ out of 5
Footwork Drills	
1. Shuffle-Slide-Shadow Footwork	___ out of 5
2. Gravity Shadow Footwork	___ out of 5
3. Sashay Step Shadow Footwork	___ out of 5
4. Footwork and Movement	___ out of 5
Racket and Bird Control Drills	
1. Handshake	___ out of 5
2. Shuttle Bounce	___ out of 10
3. Shuttle Scoop	___ out of 5
4. Shuttle Toss and Catch	___ out of 5
5. Bird Carry	___ out of 5
Total	___ *out of 55*

If you scored at least 40 out of a possible 55 points, you are ready to move on to the next step. If you scored fewer than 40 points, repeat the drills that were difficult for you. Have a coach, instructor, or experienced player evaluate your skill.

In step 2, you will learn the serve. The serve is the most important stroke in badminton. It initiates play for both the server and the receiver and potentially allows either to score on any service attempt. A properly executed serve determines to a great extent who wins the badminton match.

Serve

Because of the new scoring system, the server no longer has an automatic advantage. In fact, many players elect to receive serve because they perceive the serve as a defensive shot that must be hit below waist level with the racket head below the wrist. The shuttle must go up to be put in play, opening the chance for the receiver to rush the serve and put it away or smash it. Also the server could fault, leading to a free point for the receiver. Some of the new strategic approaches relative to choosing to serve versus receiving serve are discussed in more detail in step 9.

Think of serving in badminton as similar to being a broker in the stock market. A good stockbroker will provide good advice, and you will receive good returns on your investments. In badminton, good serves give you a better opportunity for success or to score points and win games.

In order for your serve to be legal, you must make contact with the shuttle below your waist and the racket shaft must point downward. Your entire racket head must be discernibly below any part of your racket hand before striking the shuttle.

The underhand serve puts the shuttle in play at the beginning of each rally and, therefore, is probably the most important single stroke. It is difficult to score consistently without an adequate serve. Also, players often use this stroke to set up a practice partner for practicing strokes or drills.

The long serve is the basic singles serve. This serve directs the shuttle high and deep, and the shuttle should turn over and fall as close to the back boundary line as possible. Thus the shuttle is more difficult to time and hit solidly, making all your opponent's returns less effective. The short, low serve is most often used in doubles play. Because the doubles service court is 30 inches (76 cm) shorter and 18 inches (46 cm) wider than the singles service court, the low serve seems to be more effective in doubles. This serve may be delivered from either the forehand or the backhand side. Other in-between variations are the drive and the flick serves. These good alternatives give the receiver less time on the return and may result in quick points. However, both serves are hit upward, and you should use them when they are least expected. Discussions later in this step and in steps 9 and 10 address strategies for returning these serves.

LONG SERVE

The long serve resembles a forehand underhand swinging motion. Stand near the centerline and approximately 4 to 5 feet (1.2 to 1.5 m) behind the short service line. This positions you close to centercourt and approximately equidistant from all of the corners. Your feet should be staggered up and back with your dominant foot back (figure 2.1a). The forefinger and thumb of your nondominant hand should hold the shuttle at its base, extended in front of your body about waist level. Hold your racket arm in a backswing position with your hand and wrist in a cocked position.

Misstep

You consistently serve the bird long, out of the singles court.

Correction

Move your starting position farther back so it's nearer the center of the court.

As you release the shuttle, transfer your weight from your back foot to your forward foot and pull your arm down to contact the shuttle at approximately knee height (figure 2.1b). Your forearm rotation and wrist action provide most of the power.

The follow-through is up in line with the path of the shuttle and finishes over your opposite shoulder (figure 2.1c).

Figure 2.1   Long Serve

PREPARATION

1. Apply handshake (pistol) grip
2. Perform up-and-back stance
3. Hold bird at waist level
4. Put your weight on your rear foot
5. Place your racket arm in backswing
6. Cock your wrist

a

b

c

EXECUTION

1. Shift your weight
2. Use your forearm pronation and wrist action
3. Contact at about knee level
4. Execute a high and deep serve

FOLLOW-THROUGH

1. Finish with your racket upward and in line with the bird's flight
2. Cross your racket in front of and over opposite shoulder
3. Roll your hips and shoulders around

Misstep

You often serve the bird into the net.

Correction

Angle the racket face slightly more open to direct the serve higher.

Service Drill 1. *Bird on a String*

Attach a bird to a string or cord approximately 36 inches (92 cm) long. Tie the string in an open spot between two nets. This should allow the bird to be suspended approximately knee height for a beginning server. Occasionally, beginning badminton players have trouble making contact with a shuttle being dropped from the nondominant hand on the underhand clear or singles serve. The bird on a string allows the beginner infinite opportunities to hit the bird in an underhand serving motion. The racket arm begins in the backswing position, with your hand and wrist in a cocked position. As you simulate releasing the shuttle, transfer your weight from your back foot to your forward foot and pull your arm down to contact the shuttle about knee height. The bird will fly around the net cable; you will not have to go and fetch the bird. Simply stop the shuttle from swinging around and position it for another attempt. Complete 10 forehand long serving motions.

To Increase Difficulty

- Hold the bird in the nonracket hand and drop the shuttle, attempting to contact it on its descent from your hand. Place targets in specific areas of the service court (for example, on the outside corners).
- Lengthen the string to lower the serving area or contact point.

To Decrease Difficulty

- Shorten the string to raise the serving area or contact point.

Success Check

- Begin with your feet up and back, with the racket held in a backswing position.
- Shift your weight forward as you swing.
- Contact your serve about knee high.

Score Your Success

Hit at least 10 forehand long serves using the bird on a string = 5 points

Hit 5 to 9 forehand long serves using the bird on a string = 3 points

Hit 1 to 4 forehand long serves using the bird on a string = 1 point

Your score ___

Service Drill 2. *Long Serve*

Start with the handshake grip. Stand close to the centerline and behind the short service line on your court. Serve 30 forehand long serves from each side. A good serve will land in the court diagonally opposite your service court and just past the doubles back service line or in the back alley (figure 2.2). Adjust your starting position accordingly, but attempt to serve from as close to your centercourt position as possible. If you are hitting your serves past the back boundary line, move your starting position farther back from the short service line. If you are hitting your serves consistently short, emphasize rolling your hips and shoulders into the long serve. Exaggerate the height if necessary to get the shuttle to turn over and fall in a perpendicular path as close to the back boundary line as possible.

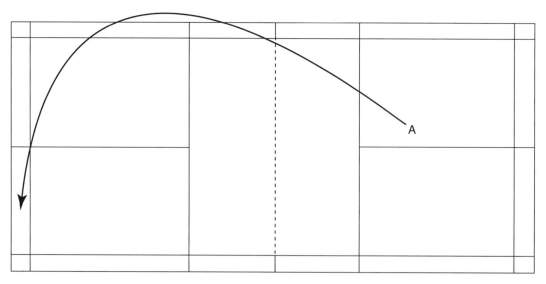

Figure 2.2 A good long serve lands in the court diagonally opposite the service court, just past the doubles back service line or in the back alley.

To Increase Difficulty

- Use a heavier racket, such as a tennis racket, for more resistance.
- Overload or increase your resistance by using a racket parachute or racket cover.
- Use a shuttle that is specifically designed to be slower (green band, blue band).

To Decrease Difficulty

- Serve from closer to the net on your side.
- Use a much lighter racket to develop more racket speed and hit the shuttle faster.
- Use a shuttle designed to be faster (red band), such as an outdoor bird.
- Drop and hit the long serve into a high, flat wall until you are consistently making good contact with the shuttle.

- Suspend a shuttle with a string from a goal or the net at your knee level. Practice your underhand long serve until you can consistently make good contact with the shuttle.

Success Check

- Stagger your feet up and back.
- Roll your hips and shoulders into the serve, rotating your forearm and wrist vigorously.
- Drive your long serve up, high, and deep.

Score Your Success

30 good forehand long serves = 10 points

20 to 29 good forehand long serves = 5 points

10 to 19 good forehand long serves = 1 point

Your score ____

SHORT SERVE

Begin the short serve with the same preparation as the long serve. The primary exception is that you should stand much closer to the short service line, perhaps within 6 inches (15 cm) or less. Your racket arm begins in a similar backswing position, with your hand and wrist in a cocked position (figure 2.3a). As you release the shuttle, transfer your weight from your back foot to your forward foot and pull your arm down to contact the shuttle below waist height. However, as your racket hand comes forward, there is little or no wrist action because the shuttle is guided or pushed over the net rather than hit (figure 2.3b). The follow-through is short with your racket finishing up and in line with the serve (figure 2.3c).

Figure 2.3   Forehand Short Serve

PREPARATION

1. Apply handshake (pistol) grip
2. Perform up-and-back stance
3. Hold bird at waist level
4. Place your racket arm in backswing position
5. Cock your wrist

a

(continued)

Figure 2.3 *(continued)*

b

c

EXECUTION

1. Shift your weight back to front
2. Use little or no wrist action
3. Contact at thigh level
4. Push or guide shuttle
5. Execute low, close to the net

FOLLOW-THROUGH

1. Finish with your racket upward in line with the bird's flight
2. Cross your racket over in front of your opposite shoulder
3. Roll your hips and shoulders around

Misstep

You consistently serve the bird too high over the net on the short serve.

Correction

Close the face of your racket to hit a flatter trajectory.

Contact the backhand short serve (figure 2.4a-c) in front of your body with a square or slightly staggered stance. The backhand short serve has several advantages:

- It travels a shorter distance.
- It gets across the net and to your opponent sooner.

- It tends to blend in with your clothing, which provides a form of camouflage.

Some players actually stand on their tiptoes to serve a higher and slightly flatter trajectory during the backhand short serve.

Figure 2.4   Backhand Short Serve

PREPARATION

1. Apply handshake (pistol) grip
2. Square or slightly stagger your stance
3. Hold bird at waist level
4. Put your weight on both feet
5. Place racket arm in backswing
6. Cock wrist

a

EXECUTION

1. Put your weight on the balls of your feet or up on your toes
2. Use little or no wrist action
3. Contact at thigh level
4. Push or guide the shuttle
5. Execute low, close to the net

b

FOLLOW-THROUGH

1. Finish with your racket upward in line with the bird's flight
2. Cross your racket over in front of the same shoulder
3. Roll your hips and shoulders around and finish with both arms up

c

Misstep

You feel intimidated and self-conscious before your serve.

Correction

Focus on the bird as long as possible. Try to see the bird hit your racket, and don't watch your opponent's body movements before serving.

Service Drill 3. *Short Serve*

Start with the handshake grip. Stand close to the centerline and close behind the short service line on your court. Serve 30 forehand short serves from each side. A good serve will land in the court diagonally opposite your service court and just past the short service line (figure 2.5). Position yourself as close to your short service line as possible. If you are hitting your serves into the net, move your starting position farther back from the short service line. If you are hitting your serves consistently short, try to emphasize hitting the shuttle more in front of you in order to shorten the distance to your opponent's court. Push, guide, or direct the shuttle into the T area (the intersection of the short service line and the centerline) which is the shortest distance. Repeat the 30 serves from the other side using the backhand short serve. When using the backhand short serve, rise on your tiptoes to serve from a higher position. This will allow you to serve the shuttle flatter and still clear the net on your short serve.

To Increase Difficulty

- Alternate short serves from near the center-line to out wide in the alley.
- Attempt to serve backhand short serves with your eyes closed. Feel the serve.

To Decrease Difficulty

- Serve from closer to the net on your side.
- Bend the elbow on your racket arm to shorten the lever and to get the shuttle closer to you.
- If your serves are falling short, use a shuttle designed to be faster (red band), such as an outdoor bird.
- If your serves are too high or too long, use a shuttle specifically designed to be slower (green band, blue band).

Success Check

- Stagger your feet up and back for forehand; square your feet for backhand.
- Drop shuttle from approximately waist high for forehand; drop in front of the racket for backhand.
- Contact serve about thigh high for forehand; hip high for backhand.

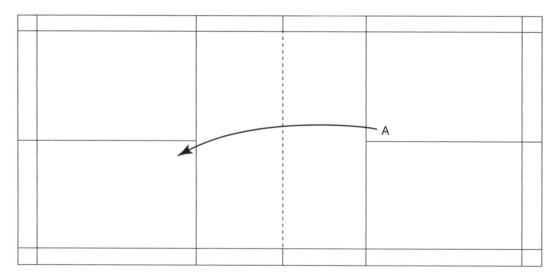

Figure 2.5 A good short serve lands opposite your service court just past the short service line.

Score Your Success

30 good forehand short serves = 10 points

20 to 29 good forehand short serves = 5 points

10 to 19 good forehand short serves = 1 point

Your score ___

30 good backhand short serves = 10 points

20 to 29 good backhand short serves = 5 points

10 to 19 good backhand short serves = 1 point

Your score ___

Your total score ___

Service Drill 4. *Under the Rope*

Attach a rope or cord approximately 18 inches (46 cm) above and parallel to the top of the net. Push or guide short serves under the rope and into the appropriate service court. Serve most of your short serves to the T, the intersection of the short service line and the centerline. This is the shortest potential distance to the receiver. The bird will get to your opponent sooner and thus give him or her less time to return it. Doing this will also give your opponent less of an angle for returns. Complete 10 forehand short serves and 10 backhand short serves. Then hit 10 additional short serves, alternating forehand and backhand.

To Increase Difficulty

- Place targets in specific areas of the service court (for example, on the outside corners).
- Lower the rope to make the serving area smaller.

To Decrease Difficulty

- Raise the rope to make the serving area larger.
- Serve from farther back from the net.

Success Check

- Begin with your feet up and back, near the short service line.
- Shift your weight forward as you swing.
- Contact your serve below your waist.

Score Your Success

Hit forehand serves under the rope and in the proper court at least 6 times = 5 points

Hit forehand serves under the rope and in the proper court 4 or 5 times = 3 points

Hit forehand serves under the rope and in the proper court 2 or 3 times = 1 point

Your score ___

Hit backhand serves under the rope and in the proper court at least 6 times = 5 points

Hit backhand serves under the rope and in the proper court 4 or 5 times = 3 points

Hit backhand serves under the rope and in the proper court 2 or 3 times = 1 point

Your score ___

Hit alternate serves under the rope and in the proper court at least 6 times = 5 points

Hit alternate serves under the rope and in the proper court 4 or 5 times = 3 points

Hit alternate serves under the rope and in the proper court 2 or 3 times = 1 point

Your score ___

Your total score ___

DRIVE AND FLICK SERVES

If your short serve is temporarily inconsistent or if your opponents are anticipating your short serve, use the drive and flick serves to keep your opponents honest.

Misstep

The receiver seems to be able to rush and put away your serve.

Correction

Mix up your serves, both in their types and in their direction or placement.

The drive serve (figure 2.6a-c) is a low, flat serve usually directed to an opponent's backhand. The advantages of the drive serve are its quickness and unexpectedness. Hold your racket arm in a backswing position with your hand and wrist in a cocked position. As you release the shuttle, transfer your weight from your back foot to your forward foot and pull your arm down to contact the shuttle below waist height. However, as your racket hand comes forward, snap your racket through with vigorous forearm rotation and wrist action. The follow-through is longer than the short serve; the racket finishes up and in line with the serve. The drive and flick serves are often delivered very close to the point of being illegal (i.e., above the waist). Players should avoid illegal drive or flick serves in which the racket head contacts the shuttle at a point above any part of the racket hand or higher than waist level.

Figure 2.6 — Drive Serve

a

b

PREPARATION

1. Apply handshake (pistol) grip
2. Perform up-and-back stance
3. Hold the bird near waist level
4. Put your weight on your rear foot
5. Place your racket arm in backswing
6. Cock your wrist

EXECUTION

1. Shift your weight
2. Use vigorous wrist action and forearm rotation
3. Contact at thigh level
4. Execute a quick, low, flat shot

FOLLOW-THROUGH

1. Finish with your racket upward in line with the bird's flight
2. Finish your swing quickly to recover in ready position
3. Finish with both of your arms up, prepared for a quick return

c

Misstep

You experience an inconsistent serve, fatigue, or lack of confidence.

Correction

Try to be in good shape and concentrate. Fatigue often causes inconsistency. Mental and physical practice will give you consistency and confidence.

The flick also resembles the short serve, but it is delivered by quickly uncocking your wrist (figure 2.7a-c). Your racket arm begins in a similar backswing, cocked position. As you release the shuttle, transfer your weight from your back foot to your forward foot and pull your arm down to contact the shuttle below waist height. However, as your racket hand comes forward, there is vigorous wrist action as the shuttle is hit higher than your opponent can reach, but not high enough for him or her to get back and make an effective return. The follow-through is longer, similar to the drive serve.

Figure 2.7 | Flick Serve

PREPARATION

1. Apply handshake (pistol) grip
2. Perform up-and-back stance
3. Hold bird at waist level
4. Put your weight on your rear foot
5. Place your racket arm in backswing
6. Cock your wrist

a

(continued)

Figure 2.7 *(continued)*

b

c

EXECUTION

1. Shift your weight
2. Use vigorous wrist action and forearm rotation
3. Contact below waist height
4. Direct shuttle higher, out of reach

FOLLOW-THROUGH

1. Finish with your racket upward in line with the bird's flight
2. Finish your swing quickly to recover in ready position
3. Finish with both of your arms up, prepared for a quick return

Misstep

The receiver stands very close, almost at the short service line, allowing the server to deliver a successful drive or flick serve.

Correction

Alter your position to receive the serve from a slightly deeper location, 2 to 3 feet (0.6 to 0.9 m) behind the short service line.

Misstep

You swing and miss the shuttle altogether on your serve.

Correction

Suspend a bird from a string and hold it at knee level. Hold the string securely or hang it from a net and take several practice swings. You may also shorten your swing, shorten your grip on the handle, or drop the bird from a lower height.

The backhand side also effectively delivers the drive and flick serves. Both backhand serves can be effective because they are delivered with a sudden change of pace and at the very last moment before contact. This adds an element of surprise because the preparation looks identical to the low, short backhand serve. This provides a deceptive quality to the backhand drive and flick serves.

Service Drill 5. *Drive and Flick Serves*

Start with the handshake grip. Stand close to the centerline and close behind the short service line on your court (figure 2.8). Serve 30 forehand drive serves and 30 forehand flick serves from each side. A good drive serve should be low and flat and land in the backhand side of your opponent's service court. A good flick serve should loop and go deep, also landing in the backhand side of your opponent's service court. Adjust your starting position accordingly, but attempt to serve from as close to your short service line as comfortable. If you are hitting serves into the net, move your starting position farther back from the short service line. If you are consistently hitting serves short, try to emphasize snapping your racket through the shuttle with a quick uncocking of the wrist. Exaggerate the height on the drive serve if necessary to get the shuttle over your opponent's reach and as close to the back boundary line as possible. Repeat the drill using the backhand.

To Increase Difficulty

- Alternate serves deep near the centerline to deep and out wide to the alley.
- Alternate forehand serves with backhand serves.
- Alternate drive and flick serves.

To Decrease Difficulty

- Serve from farther away from the net on your side.

Figure 2.8 Drive and flick serves drill.

- Use a shuttle designed to be faster (red band), such as an outdoor bird.

Success Check

- Hit the serve underhanded.
- Drop the shuttle from approximately waist height.
- Snap your racket by applying vigorous forearm rotation and wrist action into the serve.
- Contact the serve about thigh high.
- The drive serve is a quick, low, flat shot; the flick serve is looped just beyond the opponent's reach.

Score Your Success

30 good forehand drive serves = 10 points

20 to 29 good forehand drive serves = 5 points

10 to 19 good forehand drive serves = 1 point

Your score ___

30 good backhand drive serves = 10 points

20 to 29 good backhand drive serves = 5 points

10 to 19 good backhand drive serves = 1 point

Your score ___

Your total score ___

30 good forehand flick serves = 10 points

20 to 29 good forehand flick serves = 5 points

10 to 19 good forehand flick serves = 1 point

Your score ___

30 good backhand flick serves = 10 points

20 to 29 good backhand flick serves = 5 points

10 to 19 good backhand flick serves = 1 point

Your score ___

Your total score ___

Service Drill 6. *Target Serves*

Place a large cardboard box in your opponent's service court. Look at the target before you deliver the serve. Push or guide the short serve just past the short service line. Lift the high, deep serve so the bird turns over and falls perpendicular to the back boundary line. Drive and flick serves may also be directed toward targets in your opponent's service court. Complete 10 serves.

To Increase Difficulty

- Place targets in specific areas of the service court (for example, at the T area).
- Set up smaller targets (for example, a towel, a racket cover, or a smaller box).

To Decrease Difficulty

- Set up larger targets.
- Move targets to various corners of the service court.

Success Check

- Begin with your feet up and back.
- Shift your weight forward as you swing.
- Contact your serve below your waist.

Score Your Success

Hit the target 5 to 10 times = 5 points

Hit the target 3 or 4 times = 3 points

Hit the target 1 or 2 times = 1 point

Your score ____

Service Drill 7. *Over the Rope Drill*

Place two volleyball standards about halfway between the net and your opponent's back boundary line. Tie a rope, cord, or tape about 10 feet (3 m) high at the middle of your opponent's service court. Lift your long serves over the rope and into the proper service court. Serve most of your long serves into the back alley of your opponent's singles service court. The shuttle will drop almost perpendicular to the floor, which requires your opponent to move to his or her backcourt to return the serve.

To Increase Difficulty

- Place targets in the corners of the back alley of the singles service court.
- Raise the rope higher.
- Move farther back from the net.

To Decrease Difficulty

- Lower the rope.
- Move closer to the net.

Success Check

- Begin with your feet up and back, approximately 3 feet (1 m) behind the short service line.
- Shift your weight forward as you swing.
- Lift the bird high and deep.

Score Your Success

Hit serves over the rope and in the proper court at least six times = 5 points

Hit serves over the rope and in the proper court four or five times = 3 points

Hit serves over the rope and in the proper court two or three times = 1 point

Your score ____

RETURN OF SERVE

The return of serve is important because it determines your and your opponent's success in scoring points. A good return allows little chance for your opponent to score. Each service return should allow room for error and yet force your opponent into a weak return.

Return of serve should open up the court and reduce the possible angle of return by your opponent. It should also give you as much time as possible and very little time for your opponent. In singles, the return of serve should have the possibility of being directed to all four corners of the court. The service return should make your opponent move the greatest distance possible. In doubles, the return of serve should be pushed or directed toward either side alley near midcourt. This forces your opponent to hit the return upward, giving you the offensive position. Every return should be hit downward, if possible. Every service return should attempt to force an upward return by your opponent.

Misstep

You return a long serve too short or near midcourt.

Correction

Direct your return of the long serve to the four corners of your opponent's court.

Misstep

You make a clear return of the short serve or hit it up to your opponents.

Correction

Push or direct your return down either sideline past the opponent nearest the net.

Lack of practice usually causes problems with consistency and placement of the serve and service return. Few players concentrate enough on their serve and return of serve. Spend additional practice time to develop an accurate and effective serve and service return for both singles and doubles.

Serve Return Drill 1. *Four Corners Target Drill*

Player A serves high to player B who is receiving in his or her right service court (figure 2.9). Player B attempts to return the serve to one of the four corners of the singles court. Place a target, such as a towel or racket cover, in each corner as a target. You may also use trash cans as targets. Players can make a basket. The person returning the serve earns points for each target hit. After a total of 10 serves and returns, players switch sides. Player A serves high to player B who is receiving in his or her left service court. Player B attempts to return the serve to one of the four corners of player A's singles court.

Success Check

- Assess how accurately you directed returns from your right-hand service court to the four corners of the singles court by noting visually where your shots landed.

- Assess how accurately you directed returns from your left-hand service court to the four corners of the singles court by noting visually where your shots landed.

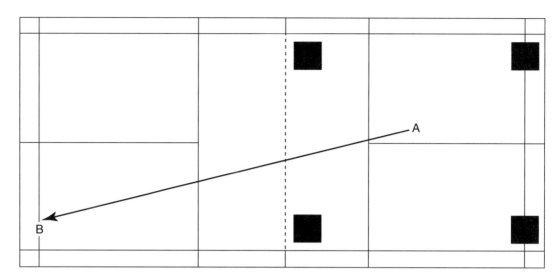

Figure 2.9 Player A serves to player B.

Score Your Success

Hit 10 targets = 5 points

Hit 7 to 9 targets = 3 points

Hit 4 to 6 targets = 1 point

Your score ___

Serve Return Drill 2. *Overhead Clear and Drop Shot Return of Serve*

Player A serves high to player B, who is receiving in his or her right service court. Player B attempts to alternate hitting returns of this serve with first a forehand overhead clear straight ahead to his or her opponent's back left corner, followed by a forehand overhead drop shot to his or her opponent's front left corner. Place a target, such as a towel or racket cover, in each corner as a target. You may also use trash cans as targets. Players can make a basket. The person returning the serve earns points for each target hit. After a total of 10 serves and returns, players switch roles. After each player has a chance to hit returns from the right singles court, expand the drill to include returns from the left court.

Success Check

- Assess how accurately you directed returns to the two corners of your opponent's right-hand side of the singles court by noting visually where your shots landed.
- Assess how accurately you directed returns to the two corners of your opponent's left-hand side of the singles court by noting visually where your shots landed.

Score Your Success

Hit 10 targets = 5 points

Hit 7 to 9 targets = 3 points

Hit 4 to 6 targets = 1 point

Your score ___

Serve Return Drill 3. *Underhand Drop Shot Return of Short Serve*

Player A serves low, short serves to player B who is receiving in his or her right service court. Player B attempts to alternate hitting returns of this serve with first an underhand drop shot return to his or her opponent's back left corner, followed by an underhand drop shot to his or her opponent's front left corner. Place a target, such as a towel or racket cover, in each corner as a target. You may also use trash cans as targets. Players can make a basket. The person returning the serve earns points for each target hit. After a total of 10 serves with 5 returns to the left and 5 returns to the right, players switch roles. Player B now serves to player A. After each player has a chance to hit returns from the right singles court, expand the drill to include returns from the left court.

Success Check

- Assess how accurately you directed returns from your right court to each corner of your opponent's doubles court by noting visually where your shots landed.
- Assess how accurately you directed returns from your left court to each corner of your opponent's doubles court by noting visually where your shots landed.

Score Your Success

Hit 10 targets = 5 points

Hit 7 to 9 targets = 3 points

Hit 4 to 6 targets = 1 point

Your score ___

Serve Return Drill 4. *Underhand Push Shot Return of Short Serve*

Player A serves low, short serves to player B who is receiving in his or her right service court. Player B attempts to alternate hitting returns of this serve with first an underhand, push shot return to his or her opponent's left midcourt, followed by an underhand push shot to his or her opponent's right midcourt. Place a target, such as a towel or racket cover, at midcourt on each side as a target. You may also use trash cans as targets. Players can make a basket. The person returning the serve earns points for each target hit. After a total of 10 serves with 5 returns to the left and 5 returns to the right, players switch roles. Player B now serves to Player A. After each player has a chance to hit returns from the right doubles court, expand the drill to include returns from the left doubles service court.

Success Check

- Assess how accurately you directed returns from your right court to each midcourt area of your opponent's doubles court by noting visually where your shots landed.
- Assess how accurately you directed returns from your left court to each midcourt area of your opponent's doubles court by noting visually where your shots landed.

Score Your Success

Hit 10 targets = 5 points

Hit 7 to 9 targets = 3 points

Hit 4 to 6 targets = 1 point

Your score ___

Serve Return Drill 5. *Overhand Smash Return of Flick Serve*

Player A flick serves to player B who is receiving in his or her right doubles service court. Player B attempts to hit returns of this serve with an overhand smash return to his or her opponent's left midcourt, followed by an overhand smash to his or her opponent's right midcourt. Place a target, such as a towel or racket bag, at midcourt on each side. You may also use carpet remnants or trash cans as targets. Players can score or make a basket. The person returning the serve earns points for each target hit. After a total of 10 serves with 5 returns to the left and 5 returns to the right, players switch roles. Player B now serves to Player A. After each player has a chance to hit returns from the right doubles court, expand the drill to include returns from the left doubles service court.

Success Check

- Assess how accurately you directed returns from your right court to each midcourt area of your opponent's doubles court by noting visually where your shots landed.
- Assess how accurately you directed returns from your left court to each midcourt area of your opponent's doubles court by noting visually where your shots landed.

To Increase Difficulty

- The receiver alternates hitting full smashes, half smashes, and fast drops.
- Set up smaller targets such as towels, racket covers, or small boxes.
- Move targets to various areas of the server's doubles court.

To Decrease Difficulty

- Allow for a larger target by allowing the shuttle to land anywhere between the short service line and the back service line for doubles.
- Set up larger targets such as bigger towels.

Score Your Success

Hit 10 targets = 5 points

Hit 7 to 9 targets = 3 points

Hit 4 to 6 targets = 1 point

Your score ___

Serve Return Drill 6. *Overhand Smash Return of Drive Serve*

Player A hits drive serves to player B who is receiving in his or her right doubles service court. Player B attempts to hit returns of this serve with an overhand smash return to his or her opponent's left midcourt, followed by an overhand smash to his or her opponent's right midcourt. Place a target, such as a towel or racket bag, at midcourt on each side. You may also use carpet remnants or trash cans as targets. Players can score or make a basket. The person returning the serve earns points for each target hit. After a total of 10 serves with 5 returns to the left and 5 returns to the right, players switch roles. Player B now serves to Player A. After each player has a chance to hit returns from the right doubles court, expand the drill to include returns from the left doubles service court.

Success Check

- Assess how accurately you directed returns from your right court to each midcourt area of your opponent's doubles court by noting visually where your shots landed.
- Assess how accurately you directed returns from your left court to each midcourt area of your opponent's doubles court by noting visually where your shots landed.

To Increase Difficulty

- The receiver must alternate hitting full smashes, half smashes, and fast drops.
- Set up smaller targets such as towels, racket covers, or small boxes.
- Move targets to various areas of the server's doubles court.

To Decrease Difficulty

- Allow for a larger target by allowing the shuttle to land anywhere between the short service line and the back service line for doubles.
- Set up larger targets such as bigger towels.

Hit 10 targets = 5 points

Hit 7 to 9 targets = 3 points

Hit 4 to 6 targets = 1 point

Your score ____

SUCCESS SUMMARY OF THE SERVE

If you can serve a variety of serves and readily mix up your service selection during a game or match, you are on your way to becoming a better badminton player. The ability to incorporate numerous different serves puts more pressure on your opponent and improves your chances of succeeding in badminton. The long, short, drive, and flick serves all provide a different look for your opponent and force him or her to play you more honestly when he or she receives your serve. Varying your serves makes them more difficult for your opponent to anticipate, and therefore increases your potential for scoring points on your serve.

Before you advance to the next step, record and tally your drill scores from this step.

Service Drills

1. Bird on a String	____ out of 5
2. Long Serve	____ out of 10
3. Short Serve	____ out of 20
4. Under the Rope	____ out of 15
5. Drive and Flick Serves	____ out of 40
6. Target Serves	____ out of 5
7. Over the Rope Drill	____ out of 5

Serve Return Drills

1. Four Corners Target Drill	___ out of 5
2. Overhead Clear and Drop Shot Return of Serve	___ out of 5
3. Underhand Drop Shot Return of Short Serve	___ out of 5
4. Underhand Push Shot Return of Short Serve	___ out of 5
5. Overhand Smash Return of Flick Serve	___ out of 5
6. Overhand Smash Return of Drive Serve	___ out of 5
Total	___ *out of 130*

If you scored at least 90 out of a possible 130 points, you are ready to move on to the next step. If you scored fewer than 70 points, repeat the drills that were difficult for you. Have a coach, instructor, or experienced player evaluate your skill.

The next step introduces the forehand and backhand overhead strokes. The overhand strokes are usually delivered from backcourt and are designed to be offensive in nature. A good overhand throwing motion is required with an emphasis on keeping the elbow up, above shoulder height. The overhand strokes are essential for success in badminton competition.

Forehand and Backhand Overhead

The overhead stroke is the most important tactical stroke in badminton play. Think of the overhead stroke as the equivalent of a professional baseball pitcher who can throw a fastball, change-up, slider, or curve ball. All four of the basic badminton shots—the clear, the smash, the drop shot, and the drive—may be delivered from the forehand or backhand sides and with an overhand action. Use both forehand and backhand strokes to move your opponent around the court.

The forehand is played with a full, throwing motion from the back half of your court. The backhand is played with a full, upward extension of your dominant arm from the backhand corner of your court and is a mirror image of the forehand stroke. If you saw a film of your forehand overhead in reverse, you would see a replica of your backhand. The extension of your arm at the elbow and vigorous forearm rotation provide most of the power for overhead strokes. Forearm pronation occurs on the forehand stroke, and forearm supination occurs on the backhand stroke. Anatomically, the forearm rotates only in these two ways. Classical wrist flexion (wrist snap) occurs very little, if at all. The proper technique allows your wrist to uncock naturally, with the racket following through in the direction of your return.

FOREHAND OVERHEAD STROKE

The forehand overhead stroke is probably the most powerful aspect of a player's game. You may employ it as an offensive or a defensive shot to move your opponent into his or her backcourt, up to the net, or to the side. A good overhead stroke from backcourt looks the same no matter what the shot. Then your opponent cannot determine which shot you are playing until after you have contacted the shuttle. If you disguise your shots well enough, the shuttle may not be returned at all. The difference between the various shots lies in the point of contact between the shuttle and your racket. Thus, the angle at which the shuttle leaves the racket and the speed of your racket at contact determine the speed of the returning shuttle.

Use the handshake grip when hitting shots on your dominant side, the right side for a right-handed player (figure 3.1a). The forehand overhead stroking motion is similar to throwing a ball. The mechanics are almost identical. When done properly, this throwing motion is the properly timed coordination of accelerations and decelerations of all body segments, producing maximum absolute velocity to your dominant hand and in turn to your racket.

Figure 3.1 Forehand Overhead Stroke

a

b

c

PREPARATION

1. Use the handshake (pistol) grip
2. Execute sideways hitting stance
3. Place both arms up
4. Put your weight on your rear foot

EXECUTION

1. Lead your elbow for arm extension
2. Move your nondominant arm down
3. Rotate your upper body
4. Reach high to hit
5. Pronate your forearm

FOLLOW-THROUGH

1. Your racket hand finishes palm out
2. Your racket finishes down in line with the bird's flight
3. Cross your racket to the opposite side of your body
4. Swing your rear foot forward with scissors action
5. Continue your weight transfer

Misstep

When you hit the overhead, the shuttle doesn't travel quickly over the net and deep into the backcourt.

Correction

Your overhead lacks power. Increase your racket speed at the top of your swing. Shift your weight forward as you swing. Use the correct grip and attempt to develop more forearm pronation and supination. You should be able to hear a swooshing sound when you swing.

Usually overhead strokes will be made from the back half of the court. As the shuttle is hit upward to your end of the court, turn your body so your feet are perpendicular to the net. Point your nondominant shoulder toward the net and shift your weight to your rear foot. If necessary, skip backward until you are slightly behind the dropping shuttle. This is your hitting stance.

As you move to the oncoming shuttle, raise your racket arm, cock your wrist, and point your racket slightly upward as your shoulders turn into your hitting position (figure 3.1*b*). When you make your stroke, several things occur very rapidly. Your forward swing begins with a drive off your rear leg, followed by hip and shoulder rotation. Extend your nonracket arm in front of your body for balance and assistance in rotating your upper body. The racket head drops down behind your head into a back-scratch position. Your dominant arm extends upward led by your elbow and vigorous rotation of your forearm and wrist. Throw your racket up to meet the shuttle with the edge of the racket leading. However, the rapid pronation of your forearm causes the racket face to rotate until it is almost flat at contact. The angle of the racket face determines the direction of the shuttle. At contact, the rapid rotation of your forearm has provided most of the power; your wrist uncocks so your arm is fully extended. Contact the shuttle at the highest possible point and in front of your body.

Misstep

Your contact point is inconsistent, resulting in a short return with little speed or power.

Correction

A common problem is failing to contact the shuttle over the racket shoulder. Instead, the shuttle is hit off to the side or behind the body. Move quickly to get behind the oncoming shuttle and keep your racket up. Concentration and hustling to get into position generally correct this problem.

Your hand and wrist allow the racket to follow through naturally, pronating and finishing downward with your racket hand rolling over, palm facing the outside. There is little or no wrist flexion (snap). Your racket travels through the contact area and then downward in line with the flight of the shuttle (figure 3.1*c*). Your racket then crosses in front of and on the opposite side of your body. Your rear foot swings forward in a scissors action continuing your weight transfer and possibly providing momentum for additional height and power.

BACKHAND OVERHEAD STROKE

The backhand overhead stroke allows you to return your opponent's shots from your backhand side even when they are completely behind you. With the proper footwork and stroking technique, your backhand saves you time and energy and can produce effective offensive or defensive shots. Some advanced players can play the majority of their returns with forehand or around-the-head returns. (See step 8 for more about around-the-head returns.) However, a player attempting to take all shots with the forehand stroke must be faster and expend more energy. The backhand overhead stroke is an excellent option and occasionally absolutely necessary. A good backhand overhead stroke looks the same no matter what shot you are attempting. Then the opponent cannot determine which shot you are playing until after you have contacted the shuttle. If you disguise your shots well enough, the shuttle may not be returned at all. As on the forehand, the difference between the various shots lies in the point of contact between the shuttle and your racket. Thus, the angle at which the shuttle leaves the racket and the speed of your racket at contact determine the speed of the returning shuttle.

Misstep

Your opponent easily reads you when you attempt to hit an overhead stroke.

Correction

Your overhead strokes lack deception. Usually this is a result of a lack of upper-body rotation. Turn your shoulders sideways to the net and give a big upper-body rotation as you throw the racket up to meet the oncoming shuttle.

The backhand overhead motion can be compared to popping a towel at the ceiling. Performing this backhand throwing motion well produces rapid extension of your dominant arm and maximum velocity to your racket head and in turn to the shuttle. These strokes will usually be made from the rear one-third of your court. As the shuttle is hit upward to your backhand, pivot and turn your body so your back is toward the net. Reach or lead with your dominant foot toward the backhand corner. Shift your weight to that rear foot. If necessary, step-close or shuffle backward until you are slightly behind the dropping shuttle. This is your hitting stance.

The backhand version of the handshake grip places your thumb straight up and down on the top left-hand bevel of the handle instead of wrapped around it (figure 3.2a). This thumb-up grip enables you to hit returns from your non-dominant side without changing your grip. It also provides added support and leverage for all backhand strokes. This is primarily a finger pressure change made by merely loosening your hold on the racket and then assuming the new hold.

Figure 3.2	**Backhand Overhead Stroke**

PREPARATION

1. Use the handshake (pistol) grip with thumb on top, left-hand bevel

2. Move sideways to your backward hitting stance

3. Hold your racket arm up with forearm parallel to the floor and your racket head pointed down

a

b

c

EXECUTION

1. Lead elbow for arm extension
2. Move your nondominant arm down
3. Rotate your upper body

CONTACT

1. Reach high to hit
2. Supinate your forearm
3. Follow through with your racket head

When you do have more time, such as on a high, deep clear to the backhand, a slight turn to the left from the recommended backhand grip provides more power. This places the knuckle of your forefinger on the top plate of the handle and your thumb diagonally across and up the back of the handle. This grip resembles the Eastern backhand grip in tennis, and it effectively locks your wrist. As long as you contact the shuttle in front of your body, this presents no problem. But in badminton play, the shuttle is often hit deep to the backhand corner, and you must hit the shuttle when it is past you or behind you. When this happens, the Eastern backhand grip becomes a liability. The recommended backhand grip covered in step 1, which is similar to the forehand grip, allows greater wrist action. It permits the face of the racket to direct the shuttle into your opponent's court even when your back is to the net and the shuttle is significantly behind you or to the side.

41

Misstep

You are unable to return the shuttle when it gets behind you on your backhand side.

Correction

An incorrect backhand grip usually causes this. Use the handshake grip. The thumb-up grip on the backhand side allows you to hit shots that are behind you.

As you move to the oncoming shuttle, raise your racket arm, cock your wrist, and point your racket slightly upward as your shoulders turn into the hitting position. When you make the stroke, several things occur very rapidly. The upward swing begins with a drive off your rear leg, followed by hip and shoulder rotation. Lift your arm from the shoulder with the forearm parallel to the floor and the racket head pointed downward (figure 3.2*b*). Extend your dominant arm upward, led by your elbow, and vigorously rotate your forearm and wrist. Throw your racket up to meet the shuttle with the racket edge leading. The rapid supination of the forearm will cause the racket face to rotate until it is almost flat at contact. The racket face angle determines the direction of the bird. At contact, the rapid rotation of your forearm provides most of the power; your wrist uncocks so your arm is fully extended. Contact the shuttle at the highest possible point, preferably in front of your body.

Misstep

You tend to short arm the return, hitting the shuttle lower than the desired height. The result is a slush return, a less powerful return that does not carry to the backcourt. This causes a loss of power and also telegraphs your intended return, allowing your opponent to anticipate where it is going well in advance.

Correction

You lack arm extension. Many beginners fail to extend their arms completely when throwing the racket upward to hit an overhead stroke. Throw your racket upward as if attempting to scrape the ceiling. Do not short arm your forehand or backhand overhead stroke.

Your hand and wrist allow your racket to follow through naturally, supinating your forearm and finishing downward (figure 3.2*c*). There is little or no wrist flexion (snap). The racket travels through the contact area and then downward in line with the return. Your rear foot pushes forward and helps you rotate around to again face the net and propel you back toward centercourt. This weight transfer may also provide added momentum and power for the shot.

Overhead Stroke Drill 1. *Racket Cover Overload*

Practice full forehand and backhand swings with the racket cover on your racket. The added weight and air resistance aid in developing strength and endurance in your hitting arm. Lead with your elbow. Complete 20 forehand swings and 20 backhand swings.

Score Your Success

Complete 20 forehand swings = 5 points

Complete 20 backhand swings = 5 points

Your score ___

Success Check

• Throw your racket.

• Extend your arm.

• Reach high.

Overhead Stroke Drill 2. *Mirror Drill*

Practice forehand and backhand overhead strokes with a full swing throwing motion while facing a mirror. The mirror will give you visual feedback. If this is not possible, practice swinging on the court. Emphasize reaching as high as possible and snapping your racket through the contact area. Make your racket swish. Complete 20 forehand swings and 20 backhand swings.

Success Check

- Shift your weight.
- Reach high.
- Swing fast.

Score Your Success

Complete 20 forehand swings = 5 points

Complete 20 backhand swings = 5 points

Your score ___

Overhead Stroke Drill 3. *Backhand Towel Drill*

Stand with your back to a high, flat wall. Grasp the end of a small towel in your dominant hand. Extend your dominant arm up with the back of your arm touching the wall. Snap the towel upward, emphasizing a vigorous rotation of your dominant arm (figure 3.3). Perform the drill for 5 minutes or 25 repetitions.

Success Check

- Flex your dominant arm at the elbow.
- Snap the towel.
- Reach high.

Score Your Success

Snap towel for 5 minutes or 25 repetitions = 5 points

Your score ___

Figure 3.3 Backhand towel drill.

Overhead Stroke Drill 4. *Wall Rally*

Practice your forehand or backhand overhead strokes by rallying with yourself against a high, flat wall (figure 3.4). Stand approximately 5 to 7 feet (1.5 to 2.1 m) from the wall and begin with an underhand return designed to rebound high off the wall requiring an overhead return. This high, overhand return should provide enough time to prepare before each hit. Lead with your elbow and drive the shuttle upward and high against the wall. Turn and get your racket back. Hit forehand strokes for 2 minutes then hit backhand strokes for 2 minutes.

Figure 3.4 Wall rally drill.

Success Check

- Hold your racket back and up.
- Rotate your shoulders, elbow leads.
- Hit high and deep.

Score Your Success

Hit forehand strokes for 2 minutes = 5 points

Hit backhand strokes for 2 minutes = 5 points

Your score _____

Overhead Stroke Drill 5. *Self-Toss Overhead Clear Return*

Because this drill is not a rally, begin with five or six shuttles. Stand sideways near the backcourt. Place a shuttle on your racket face, with your racket hand held palm up. Toss the shuttle upward with a lifting motion, putting the shuttle in position for either a forehand or backhand overhead stroke. After the shuttle leaves your racket, quickly lift your arm from the shoulder, placing your racket head downward at the end of your backswing. Extend your racket arm upward, leading with the elbow. Vigorously rotate your forearm and wrist, propelling the racket up to meet the shuttle at the highest possible point of contact. Shift your weight from your back foot to your front foot. Your racket face should direct the shuttle up and out, and your hand leads the racket before contacting the shuttle. Good returns land near or beyond the doubles service line in the backcourt. Execute 20 forehand returns and 20 backhand returns, gathering the shuttles when necessary.

To Increase Difficulty

- Recover to the ready position after each attempt.

- Alternate hitting forehand and backhand shots.
- Move toward the net and touch the short service line after each attempt and then recover to the backcourt.
- Use a tennis racket instead of a badminton racket. The increased weight provides more of an overload.

To Decrease Difficulty

- Have your body already turned in a sideways hitting stance.
- Begin with your racket already pointing upward.
- Begin with your weight already shifted to the front foot.

Success Check

- Point elbow upward with racket pointed downward.
- Lead your racket with your hand upward toward the shuttle.
- Swing fast.

Score Your Success

Hit 20 good forehand returns = 5 points

Hit 15 to 19 good forehand returns = 3 points

Hit 10 to 14 good forehand returns = 1 point

Your score ___

Score Your Success

Hit 20 good backhand returns = 5 points

Hit 15 to 19 good backhand returns = 3 points

Hit 10 to 14 good backhand returns = 1 point

Your score ___

Your total score ___

Overhead Stroke Drill 6. *High Serve and Overhead Return*

Player A serves a high, deep serve crosscourt to player B. Player B clears straight ahead with a forehand overhead throwing action (figure 3.5). Player E, who is stationed in the backcourt, returns the shuttle to player A. Rotate positions after three attempts. Player A takes the place of player E, player B replaces player A, and player E moves behind player D, and so on until all players have been at each position. Drill is repeated until each player has a minimum of six attempts. If court space is limited, two groups may be stationed on a single court.

Success Check

• Point elbow upward with your racket pointed downward.

• Lead your elbow for the initial extension of your arm.

• Lead your racket with your hand upward toward the shuttle.

Score Your Success

Hit five or more good forehand overhead returns = 5 points

Hit three or four good forehand overhead returns = 3 points

Hit one or two good forehand overhead returns = 1 point

Your score ___

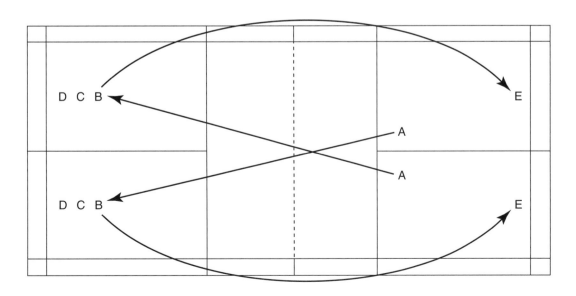

Figure 3.5 High serve and overhead return drill.

Overhead Stroke Drill 7. *Touch Tag*

This is a lead-up game for beginners. Place a mat or carpet square at the center of one side of the court. Player A stands on this side in the back forehand corner. Player B hits a high, deep serve to player A's forehand corner. Player A clears straight ahead back to player B and then attempts to run and touch the mat (figure 3.6). Player A returns to the forehand corner and the rally continues. Player B again returns straight ahead back to player A. Player A returns again to player B and again runs to touch the mat. Repeat the sequence a third time and then switch positions.

To Increase Difficulty

- Player B may lower the height of his or her return to give player A less time to recover.

To Decrease Difficulty

- Player B may raise the height of his or her return to give player A more time to recover.

Success Check

- Lead your elbow for the initial extension of your arm.
- Swing fast.
- Place shot high and deep.

Score Your Success

Hit three good forehand overhead returns = 5 points

Hit two good forehand overhead returns = 3 points

Hit one good forehand overhead return = 1 point

Your score ___

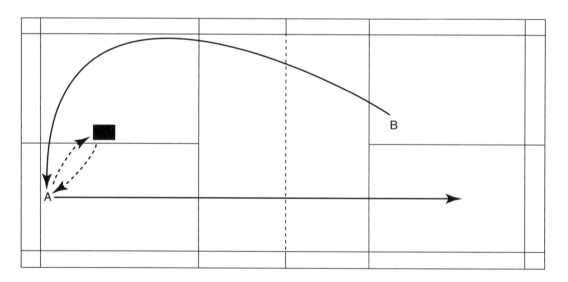

Figure 3.6   Touch tag.

Overhead Stroke Drill 8. *Shuttle Clears*

Player A hits a high, underhand clear and runs to the opposite end of the court behind player E (figure 3.7). Sequence continues with each player clearing the shuttle from his or her forehand or backhand and running to the end of the line on the opposite end of the court. Try to hit 20 good forehand overhead clears in succession and 20 good backhand clears in succession.

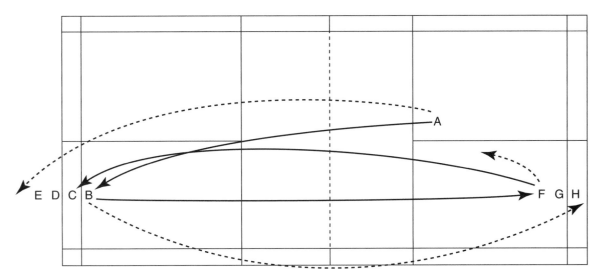

Figure 3.7 Shuttle clears.

Success Check

- Point your elbow upward with your racket pointed downward.
- Lead your elbow for the initial extension of your arm.
- Lead your racket by your hand upward toward the shuttle.

Score Your Success

Hit 20 good forehand returns = 10 points

Hit 15 to 19 good forehand returns = 5 points

Hit 10 to 14 good forehand returns = 1 point

Your score ___

Hit 20 good backhand returns = 10 points

Hit 15 to 19 good backhand returns = 5 points

Hit 10 to 14 good backhand returns = 1 point

Your score ___

Your total score ___

Overhead Stroke Drill 9. *Backhand Clears*

This drill requires a hitter and a tosser or coach. Player A hits high backhand clears as the tosser or coach feeds the bird to player A. Player A begins at a position near the back doubles service line. The coach tosses the shuttle underhand. The shuttle is looped higher than the hitter's shoulder and slightly behind him or her. Player A moves toward the backhand corner leading with his or her dominant foot. The player clears the shuttle from his or her backhand and then returns to midcourt. Player A should attempt to hit 20 good backhand clears in succession.

Success Check

- Check for the correct backhand grip.

- Point your elbow upward with your racket pointed downward.
- Lead your elbow for the initial extension of your arm.
- Lead your racket by your hand upward toward the shuttle.

Score Your Success

Hit 20 good backhand returns = 20 points

Hit 15 to 19 good backhand returns = 15 points

Hit 10 to 14 good backhand returns = 10 points

Your score ___

SUCCESS SUMMARY OF THE FOREHAND AND BACKHAND OVERHEAD

When hitting an overhead, remember to turn sideways to the net and roll your hips and shoulders into your stroke. The forehand overhead stroke should feature a smooth transition from weight shift to vigorous upper-body rotation, followed by arm extension and pronation, and finishing with your racket snapping through the shuttle at contact. Allow your hand and racket to follow through naturally. Complete the stroke by swinging your racket leg through in a scissors movement.

When hitting a backhand overhead, remember to turn backward to the net and roll your hips and shoulders into the stroke. The backhand overhead stroke should have a smooth transition from weight shift to vigorous upper-body rotation. This is followed by arm extension and supination and finished with your racket snapping through the shuttle at contact. Allow your hand and racket to follow through naturally. Complete the stroke by pushing off and propelling yourself back toward midcourt.

Practice until your overhead is a continuous, rhythmic motion that results in an effective, accurate, and powerful stroke. Before you advance to the next step, record and tally your drill scores from this step.

Overhead Stroke Drills

1. Racket Cover Overload	___ out of 10
2. Mirror Drill	___ out of 10
3. Backhand Towel Drill	___ out of 5
4. Wall Rally	___ out of 10
5. Self-Toss-Overhead Clear Return	___ out of 5
6. High Serve and Overhead Return	___ out of 5
7. Touch Tag	___ out of 5
8. Shuttle Clears	___ out of 20
9. Backhand Clears	___ out of 20
Total	___ *out of 90*

If you scored at least 70 out of a possible 90 points, you are ready to move on to the next step. If you scored fewer than 70 points, repeat the drills that were difficult for you. Have a coach, instructor, or experienced player evaluate your skill.

Step 4 introduces the clear. This high, deep return is an essential shot for successful badminton play. An age-old adage in football is "When in doubt, punt." Similarly, in badminton, you could say, "When in doubt, clear." This stroke directs the shuttle toward the backcourt. It can be defensive in nature, designed to give you time to recover, or offensive, an attacking clear that travels lower and quicker, giving your opponent less time.

Clear

The most-often recommended strategy to gain time to return to centercourt is the high deep clear. When in doubt, clear, particularly in singles play. The defensive clear is a high return that has a trajectory similar to a lob in tennis. The clear may be hit with an underhand or overhand stroke from either the forehand or backhand to force the opponent deep into the backcourt. Players use the clear in combination with the drop shot to force their opponents to run and defend all four corners of the court.

Always try to hit the bird as soon as possible so your opponent has less time to get to his or her shot. Hit overhead and underhand returns at the highest possible contact point. As you move into position to hit the clear, throw your racket upward, meeting the shuttle with a flat racket with your elbow extending. Because the shuttle should go high and deep, swing your racket forward and up with your hand leading. Then your follow-through finishes in the direction of the bird's flight.

The primary value of the clear during competition is to keep the shuttle away from your opponent and to make him or her move quickly. If you can get the bird behind your opponent or make him or her move more rapidly than he or she would like, your opponent will have less time and will become more fatigued. If you clear correctly, your opponent will need to hurry to execute his or her returns accurately and effectively. The offensive clear is a flatter, faster clear, which is useful in getting the shuttle behind your opponent and potentially causing him or her to hit weak returns. The defensive clear has a high and deep trajectory.

FOREHAND CLEAR

When the shuttle is hit to you during a rally, move into a position behind the oncoming shuttle and assume your handshake grip. If you are returning with a forehand overhead clear (figure 4.1), turn your shoulders and pivot at your waist to get sideways to the net. As the shuttle drops in the hitting area, swing your racket upward to contact the shuttle, directing it high and deep. Contact the shuttle in front of your body and as high as possible with the racket finishing in the direction of the shuttle's trajectory. The defensive clear is directed upward, high over your opponent's head. The offensive clear follows a flatter, faster trajectory just out of your opponent's reach.

Your hand and wrist allow your racket arm to follow-through naturally. Rapid forearm pronation provides most of the power. Your racket travels through the contact area and then forward in line with the flight of the shuttle. At or very soon after contact on the overhead or underhand clear, transfer your body weight rapidly as your feet push your body back toward midcourt.

Figure 4.1   Overhead Forehand Clear

a   *b*   *c*

PREPARATION

1. Apply the handshake, or pistol, grip
2. Recover into waiting or receiving stance
3. Hold your racket arm up with your racket head up
4. Distribute your weight evenly on both feet
5. Move your wrist to laid back, or cocked, position

EXECUTION

1. Pivot and turn in the direction of the shuttle
2. Swing forward to contact as high as possible
3. Pronate your forearm

FOLLOW-THROUGH

1. Follow through with your racket head
2. Swing toward the net
3. Rotate your racket arm
4. Push off back toward midcourt
5. Return to centercourt

Misstep

You use a frying pan grip, grasping the racket as if holding a pan while cooking.

Correction

The frying pan grip significantly limits power and allows only for elbow extension, resulting in a patty-cake type of hit. Grasp the racket as if shaking hands with it. The thumb and forefinger of the dominant hand form the shape of a V on top of the handle or grip. Check for this V on top.

If you are clearing from near the net, you should use an underhand stroke (figure 4.2). Reach with your dominant arm and place the racket face under the dropping return. As the shuttle drops in the hitting area, swing your racket upward to contact the shuttle, directing it high and deep. Contact the shuttle with your racket hand, palm up, in front of your body and as high as possible, directing the shuttle upward, high, and deep. Your racket finishes in the direction of the shuttle's trajectory.

Figure 4.2 | Underhand Forehand Clear

PREPARATION

1. Apply forehand hand-shake, or pistol, grip

2. Reach with your dominant hand and foot

3. Move your racket arm up with palm pointed upward

4. Put your weight slightly on your front foot

a

EXECUTION

1. Pivot and reach for the oncoming shuttle

2. Place your racket under the dropping shuttle

3. Put your wrist in laid back, or cocked, position

4. Drop your racket down and swing it up

5. Contact the shuttle as high as possible

6. Pronate your forearm

b

(continued)

Figure 4.2 *(continued)*

FOLLOW-THROUGH

1. Continue swing up with shuttle's flight
2. Rotate your forearm
3. Push off with your feet
4. Propel yourself back toward midcourt
5. Return to centercourt

c

Misstep

Your preparatory position is poor, so you are off balance and do not transfer your weight into the shot.

Correction

Move quickly to get into the proper hitting position and make contact at the proper time. You can correct this problem with concentration and practice.

BACKHAND CLEAR

When the shuttle is hit to your backhand side during a rally, you should move into a position behind the oncoming shuttle and assume your backhand grip. If you are returning with a backhand overhead clear (figure 4.3), turn your shoulders and pivot at your waist to get sideways to the net. As the shuttle drops in the hitting area, swing your racket upward with the elbow leading the hand up to contact with the shuttle. Contact the shuttle in front of your body and as high as possible with the racket finishing in the direction of the shuttle's trajectory. The racket face is angled upward, directing the shuttle high and deep. The defensive clear is directed upward, high over your opponent's head. The offensive clear is hit in a flat, fast trajectory, just out of your opponent's reach.

Your hand and wrist allow your racket arm to follow through naturally. Rapid forearm supination provides the majority of the power. Your racket travels through the contact area and then forward in line with the flight of the shuttle. At or very soon after contact on the backhand overhead, transfer your body weight rapidly as your feet push your body back toward midcourt.

Figure 4.3	Overhead Backhand Clear

a

b

c

PREPARATION

1. Apply backhand, or thumb-up, grip
2. Recover into waiting or receiving stance
3. Hold your racket arm parallel to the floor
4. Point your racket head downward
5. Distribute your weight evenly on both feet

EXECUTION

1. Reach with your dominant foot
2. Pivot and turn with your back to the net
3. Move your wrist to laid back, or cocked, position
4. Lead your elbow to a forward swing
5. Trail your racket head up to contact
6. Contact as high as possible
7. Angle racket face up and outward
8. Supinate your forearm

FOLLOW-THROUGH

1. Continue swing upward
2. Follow flight of shuttle with racket
3. Swing toward the net
4. Follow through naturally with racket
5. Push off rear foot back to midcourt
6. Return to centercourt

Misstep

Your overhead backhand clear lacks power.

Correction

A lack of power is often the result of not fully extending the arm at contact. Many beginners hit with a bent, or short arm, resulting in little or no forearm rotation. Do not short arm your throwing motion.

If you are clearing from near the net, you should use an underhand stroke (figure 4.4). Reach with your dominant arm and place the racket face under the dropping return. As the shuttle drops in the hitting area, swing your racket upward to contact the shuttle, directing it high and deep. Contact the shuttle with your racket hand, palm down, in front of your body and as high as possible. Hit the shuttle with vigorous forearm supination directing it up, high, and deep, with the racket finishing in the direction of the shuttle's trajectory.

Figure 4.4 — Underhand Backhand Clear

a

b

PREPARATION

1. Apply backhand, or thumb-up, grip
2. Reach forward with your dominant hand and foot
3. Hold your racket arm up, palm down
4. Place your weight slightly on your front foot

EXECUTION

1. Pivot and turn toward the oncoming shuttle
2. Move toward the net
3. Step with nondominant foot

SWING

1. Place your racket under dropping shuttle
2. Put your wrist in laid back, or cocked, position
3. Drop your racket down and swing it quickly up to contact the shuttle as high as possible
4. Swing up in line with shuttle's flight
5. Follow through naturally with forearm rotation
6. Push off and propel back toward mid-court
7. Return to centercourt

c

Errors in performing the clear shot are apparent at all levels of badminton competition. Beginners and often the intermediate levels demonstrate poor stroke production. Practice and repetition will provide you with more success on the court.

Clear Drill 1. *Underhand Clear Shadow*

Practice both the forehand and backhand underhand swinging motions with the racket cover on your racket. The added weight and air resistance aid in developing strength and endurance in your hitting arm. Complete 30 forehand swings and 30 backhand swings.

Success Check

• Apply wrist in cocked, or laid back, position.

• Lead with your wrist and hand. The racket trails on the upward swing.
• Make the racket swish.

Score Your Success

Complete 30 forehand swings = 5 points
Complete 30 backhand swings = 5 points
Your score ___

Clear Drill 2. *Overhand Clear Shadow*

Practice both the forehand and backhand overhand clear throwing motions with the racket cover on your racket. The added weight and air resistance aid in developing strength and endurance in your hitting arm. Complete 30 forehand swings and 30 backhand swings.

Success Check

• Lead with your elbow.

• Lead your racket with your hand on the upward swing.
• Shift your weight.

Score Your Success

Complete 30 forehand swings = 5 points
Complete 30 backhand swings = 5 points
Your score ___

Clear Drill 3.   *Underhand Clear From Net*

Player A throws the shuttle with an overhand toss just over the net toward player B, who steps toward the net with his or her dominant foot and hits an underhand clear from his or her forehand or backhand side. These underhand clear returns should land between the doubles back service line and the back boundary line (figure 4.5). Player G returns the shuttles to player A. Players rotate after three attempts. Player A replaces player G, player B replaces player A, and player G moves behind player F. Rotate through the drill five times until each player has a chance to hit 15 underhand clears.

Success Check

- Lead with your elbow.
- Swing fast.
- Place shot high and deep.

Score Your Success

Hit 15 good underhand clears = 10 points

Hit 10 to 14 good underhand clears = 5 points

Hit 5 to 9 good underhand clears = 1 point

Your score ___

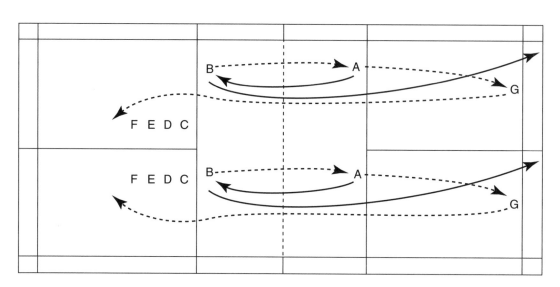

Figure 4.5   Underhand clear from net drill.

Clear Drill 4.   *Serve and Clear*

Because this drill is not a rally, the serving partner needs to begin with five or six shuttles. Start with either a forehand or backhand serve or an underhand stroking motion that results in a high, deep clear return over your partner's head. Execute 20 forehand serves or underhand clears and 20 backhand serves or underhand clears, gathering the shuttles as necessary. Because there is no rally, partners may practice this drill simultaneously or you can practice this drill solo. Good

serves need to carry over your partner's head and land near or beyond the doubles service line in the backcourt.

Success Check

- Lead with your elbow.
- Swing fast.
- Place shot high and deep.

Score Your Success

Hit 20 good forehand serves or underhand clears = 5 points

Hit 15 to 19 good forehand serves or underhand clears = 3 points

Hit 10 to 14 good forehand serves or underhand clears = 1 point

Your score ___

Hit 20 good backhand serves or underhand clears = 5 points

Hit 15 to 19 good backhand serves or underhand clears = 3 points

Hit 10 to 14 good backhand serves or underhand clears = 1 point

Your score ___

Your total score ___

Clear Drill 5. *Return Forehand Clear*

This drill is not a rally so the partner who is setting up the other needs to begin with five or six shuttles. One partner sets up the other by hitting high, deep, friendly underhand serves. The receiving partner returns each serve with a forehand overhead stroking motion (figure 4.6) that results in a high, deep clear return over his or her partner's head. The receiving partner executes at least 30 returns before the partners reverse roles. Good returns need to land near or beyond the doubles service line in the backcourt.

Success Check

- Lead with your elbow.
- Swing fast.
- Place shot high and deep.

Score Your Success

Hit 30 good forehand clears = 10 points

Hit 20 to 29 good forehand clears = 5 points

Hit 10 to 19 good forehand clears = 1 point

Your score ___

Figure 4.6 Return forehand clear drill.

57

Clear Drill 6. *Toss and Return Backhand Clear*

This drill is not a rally so the partner setting up the other needs to begin with five or six shuttles. One partner sets up the other by throwing friendly, overhand tosses to his or her partner's backhand side close to the net. The receiving partner returns each toss with a backhand underhand stroking motion, resulting in a high, deep clear return. Good returns need to land near or beyond the doubles service line in the backcourt (figure 4.7). The receiving partner should execute at least 30 returns before the partners reverse roles.

Success Check

- Toss bird to left and reach with your dominant hand and foot.
- Lead with your elbow.
- Snap the racket through the contact area.

Score Your Success

Hit 30 good backhand clears = 10 points

Hit 20 to 29 good backhand clears = 5 points

Hit 10 to 19 good backhand clears = 1 point

Your score ___

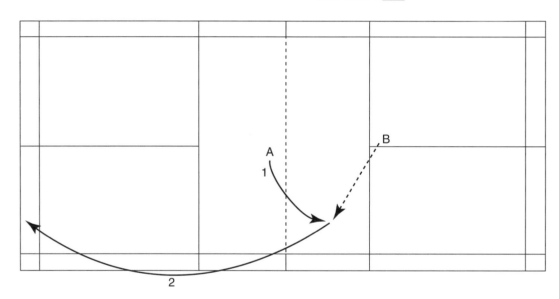

Figure 4.7 Toss and return backhand clear drill.

Clear Drill 7. *Overhead Clears Rally*

This drill is a rally so the partner setting up needs to begin with only one or two shuttles. One partner sets up the other by hitting a high, deep, friendly underhand serve. The receiving partner returns the serve with a forehand or backhand overhead stroking motion, resulting in a high, deep clear return over his or her partner's head. This is a continuous drill in which both partners should attempt to execute as many return clears as possible, keeping the rally going indefinitely. Returns should be high and deep enough to allow the other partner plenty of time to get into position. Good returns need to travel or carry near or beyond the doubles service line in the backcourt.

To Increase Difficulty

- Recover to ready position after each attempt.
- Alternate hitting forehand and backhand overhead clears.
- Run in and touch the short service line between clears, and then return to receiving position.
- Hit clears with a faster and flatter trajectory. Hit this faster, attacking clear sooner and more in front of you. Hit it high enough so your opponent cannot intercept it before it gets to the back of his or her court.

To Decrease Difficulty

- Have your body already turned in the sideways hitting stance either at the net or backcourt.
- Begin with your racket arm already held up and behind your head if you are in the backcourt or up and reaching forward if at the net.
- Begin with your weight already shifted to your rear foot if in the backcourt or to your front foot if at the net.
- Hit higher and shorter to give your partner more time. This also enables him or her to hit a deeper return to you.

Success Check

- Lead with your elbow.
- Swing fast.
- Direct return to your partner's forehand side.

Score Your Success

Hit 30 or more good clears during a rally without dropping the shuttle = 10 points

Hit 20 to 29 good clears during a rally without dropping the shuttle = 5 points

Hit 10 to 19 good clears during a rally without dropping the shuttle = 1 point

Your score ___

Clear Drill 8. *Rotating Clear*

Player A serves high to player E and rotates to the rear of his or her line (figure 4.8). Player E clears to player B and rotates to the end of his or her line. Continue with each player hitting one clear and rotating to the end of the line.

Score Your Success

Hit 30 or more good clears without dropping the shuttle = 10 points

Hit 20 to 29 good clears without dropping the shuttle = 5 points

Hit 10 to 19 good clears without dropping the shuttle = 1 point

Your score ___

Success Check

- Lead with your elbow.
- Swing fast.
- Direct return to partner's forehand side.

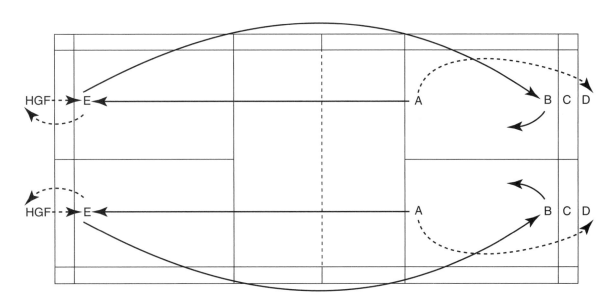

Figure 4.8 Rotating clear drill.

Clear Drill 9. *Straight and Crosscourt Clears*

You can use this sequence of clears effectively for warming up before a match. Either player may begin the drill by clearing crosscourt to his or her partner's deep forehand. After that initial clear, either partner must hit a clear return crosscourt or down the line (figure 4.9). There is no set sequence of returns, except all returns must be cleared deep, whether to your partner's forehand or backhand.

Success Check

- Lead with your elbow.
- Swing fast.
- Place shot high and deep.

Score Your Success

Hit 30 or more good clears during a rally without dropping the shuttle = 10 points

Hit 20 to 29 good clears during a rally without dropping the shuttle = 5 points

Hit 10 to 19 good clears during a rally without dropping the shuttle = 1 point

Your score ___

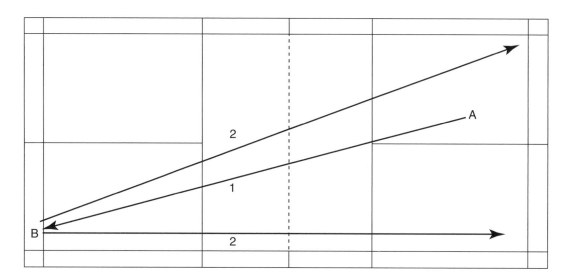

Figure 4.9 Straight and crosscourt clears drill.

SUCCESS SUMMARY OF THE CLEAR

Remember to prepare quickly to hit forehand and backhand clears. Make contact with the shuttle as soon as possible in front of your dominant shoulder. These strokes should feature a rapid weight shift followed by a quick change of direction back to midcourt. Swing your racket arm up, leading with your elbow as you extend your arm. Allow your hand and racket to follow through naturally. Complete the stroke by pushing off and propelling yourself back to midcourt with your rear foot.

Practice the overhead and underhand clears until you have a continuous, rhythmic motion that results in an effective, accurate, and powerful stroke. Attempt to visualize each stroke and critique your thoughts out loud with your coach, instructor, or experienced player. Before you advance to the next step, record and tally your drill scores from this step.

Clear Drills

1. Underhand Clear Shadow	___ out of 10
2. Overhand Clear Shadow	___ out of 10
3. Underhand Clear From Net	___ out of 10
4. Serve and Clear	___ out of 10
5. Return Forehand Clear	___ out of 10
6. Toss and Return Backhand Clear	___ out of 10
7. Overhead Clears Rally	___ out of 10
8. Rotating Clear	___ out of 10
9. Straight and Crosscourt Clears	___ out of 10
Total	___ **out of 90**

If you scored at least 65 out of a possible 90 points, you are ready to move on to the next step. If you scored fewer than 65 points, repeat the drills that were difficult for you. Have a coach, instructor, or experienced player evaluate your skill.

Step 5 covers the drop shot. The drop shot has several variations but it is essentially a return just over the net, preferably inside of the short service line and as close to the net as possible. This off-speed shot gives your opponent little time and requires him or her to advance forward near the net to make a potential return. This provides the opportunity to place your next return high and deep, forcing your opponent to retreat to backcourt in order to retrieve your shot.

Drop Shot

The drop shot is hit low, just over the net, and slow, so the bird drops directly down toward the floor after it passes over the net. The bird is contacted farther in front of the body than the overhead clear, and your racket face is angled to direct the bird more downward. The shuttle is blocked rather than hit with power.

The most important characteristic of a good overhead drop shot is deception. If you are deceptive enough, the drop shot may not be returned at all. The worst characteristic of the drop shot is its slow flight. Anything moving slowly, unfortunately, gives your opponent more time.

Emphasize making your preparatory motion similar to your other overhead strokes.

Use a big upper-body turn even though it is not necessary for generating any power. This exaggerated shoulder rotation adds to your deception. However, because the bird is blocked or sliced rather than patted, it loses speed quickly and falls straight down after passing over the net.

The value of the overhead or underhand drop shot lies in combining it with the clear to move your opponent around and force him or her to defend the entire court. To be effective, the drop shot must be directed toward one of the four corners of the court to make your opponent cover as much of his or her court as possible.

FOREHAND DROP SHOT

The intention of the forehand overhead drop shot should be to suggest that you are about to hit an overhead clear or smash. The difference is primarily in racket speed. To execute a good forehand overhead drop shot, you should assume the handshake grip and move into position behind and in line with the shuttle (figure 5.1a). As you move into position, pivot at your waist and turn your shoulders sideways to the net.

Throw your racket up to meet the shuttle. Take the overhead drop shot as high as possible and out in front of your body.

Direct the shuttle downward. Swing your racket upward with your racket head leading (figure 5.1b). Follow through in the direction of the bird's flight and finish with your racket head pointing downward (figure 5.1c). Tilt your racket face at the angle that the shuttle is to take.

Figure 5.1   Overhead Forehand Drop Shot

a   *b*   *c*

PREPARATION

1. Apply the handshake grip
2. Recover into waiting, or receiving, stance
3. Hold your arm up
4. Use your backswing to place your wrist in cocked position
5. Distribute your weight evenly on the balls of your feet

EXECUTION

1. Pivot and turn to the oncoming shuttle
2. Swing forward to contact shuttle high
3. Reach your racket out to meet the shuttle, which is blocked, not hit
4. Move your racket head so that it travels in the shuttle's direction

FOLLOW-THROUGH

1. Continue in line with the shuttle's flight
2. Allow your swing to follow the angle of the shuttle
3. Push off with your feet back toward midcourt
4. Return to centercourt

Misstep

You are telegraphing your drop shot by not turning your shoulders and hitting with vigorous upper-body rotation.

Correction

Begin in a sideways, hitting position. As you throw your racket up to meet the oncoming shuttle, extend your racket arm completely as you reach up to make contact and rotate your upper body.

Misstep

You have little or no deception. Your returns are very easy to predict.

Correction

Assume a sideways preparatory stance. Your preparation and upper-body movement should be the same for all overhead shots.

Hit the crosscourt drop shot with the same overhead motion except tilt the racket face slightly to hit more across the bird. This creates a slicing action similar to the slice serve in tennis and is intended to deceive your opponent. This deception or misdirection is sometimes difficult to pick up and may result in a winner. It is very important to begin your throwing motion with the shoulders turned sideways to the net. This is essential for deception. Also, do not short arm or bend the elbow during execution. This alerts your opponent that a drop shot is coming.

If you are hitting from near the net, use an underhand stroke (figure 5.2). Reach with the dominant arm and place the racket face under the dropping return. As the shuttle drops in the hitting area, softly bump or lift the shuttle over as close to the top of the net as possible. Contact the shuttle with your racket, hand palm up, in front of your body and as high as possible, directing the shuttle upward. Your racket finishes in a lifting motion in the direction of the shuttle's trajectory. The sooner you make contact, the better your results will be. Lift from your shoulder and not from your hand or wrist. The shuttle bounces off the face of the racket and literally falls over the net from lack of speed. The best drop shot return is the one that gets over the net the fastest and then begins to fall toward the floor on the opponent's side. Therefore, the sooner you get to the shuttle at the net, the less time your opponent will have to retrieve your return drop shot at the net.

Figure 5.2   Underhand Forehand Drop Shot

PREPARATION

1. Apply the forehand handshake grip
2. Reach with your dominant hand and foot
3. Hold your racket arm up
4. Put your weight slightly on your front foot

a

EXECUTION

1. Pivot and reach in the direction of shuttle

2. Place your racket under the dropping shuttle

3. Put your wrist in laid back, or cocked, position

4. Drop your racket down and lift to contact shuttle as high as possible

5. Lift from your shoulder; bump shuttle over the net

b

FOLLOW-THROUGH

1. Use a short swing up with the shuttle's flight

2. Allow your racket to tumble shuttle over net

3. Push off with your feet back toward midcourt

c

 Misstep

Your drop shot return is too high, allowing your opponent more time to get to the shot and potentially put it away. Or you hit the shot too softly and it fails to get over the net.

Correction

Many beginners fail to work on their feel or touch. Practice the drop shot from backcourt and at the net.

You may also slice or tumble the shuttle over the net to make it more difficult for your opponent to return this hairpin net drop. Another variation of the drop shot hit at the net is the push shot. Play the push shot at or above the top of the net and direct the shuttle down into your opponent's court. This is particularly effective in doubles play when you push the shuttle past the net player and force the backcourt player to hit his or her return up. There may also be some indecision as to which player should make the return. The sooner and higher you contact the shuttle, the sharper and steeper your net returns will be.

BACKHAND DROP SHOT

When the shuttle is hit to your backhand side during a rally, move into position behind the oncoming shuttle and assume a backhand grip. If you are returning with a backhand overhead drop shot, turn your shoulders and pivot at your waist to get sideways to the net. As the shuttle drops in the hitting area, swing your racket up with the elbow leading the hand up to contact the shuttle (figure 5.3). Contact the shuttle in front of your body and as high as possible; the racket finishes in the direction of the shuttle's trajectory. Angle the racket face downward, directing the shuttle close to the top of the net.

Your hand and wrist allow your racket arm to follow through naturally. Forearm supination provides most of the power. Your racket travels through the contact area and then forward in line with the flight of the shuttle. However, because the bird is blocked or sliced rather than patted, it loses speed quickly and falls straight down after passing over the net. At or soon after contact on the backhand overhead drop shot, transfer your body weight rapidly as your feet push your body back toward midcourt.

| Figure 5.3 | **Overhead Backhand Drop Shot** |

PREPARATION

1. Apply backhand, or thumb-up, grip
2. Recover into waiting or receiving stance
3. Hold racket arm parallel to floor
4. Point racket head downward
5. Distribute weight evenly on both feet

a

b

c

EXECUTION

1. Reach with your dominant foot
2. Pivot and turn back to net
3. Use backswing to place wrist in cocked position
4. Lead forward swing with your elbow
5. Allow racket head to lead hand up to contact
6. Contact as high as possible
7. Angle racket face downward
8. Supinate forearm

FOLLOW-THROUGH

1. Continue swing down with shuttle's flight
2. Swing toward net
3. Push off your rear foot back to midcourt
4. Return to centercourt

Misstep

Your preparatory position is poor. The racket arm is not fully extended.

Correction

Move quickly to get into the proper hitting position and make contact as soon as possible, but under control. The racket face must be angled slightly upward to create a return that travels in a rainbow trajectory, up and then down. Extend the racket arm fully and contact the shuttle with the racket face angled downward to send the shuttle in a path traveling only down into your opponent's court.

If you are hitting a drop shot at the net, you should use an underhand stroke. Reach with the dominant arm and place the racket face under the dropping return. As the shuttle drops in the hitting area, lift your racket upward to contact the shuttle, bumping it just over the net (figure 5.4). Contact the shuttle with your racket, hand palm down, in front of your body and as high as possible. Hit the shuttle with a lifting motion from the shoulder with very little follow-through. The racket finishes in the direction of the shuttle's trajectory.

Figure 5.4 — Underhand Backhand Drop Shot

PREPARATION

1. Use backhand, or thumb-up, grip
2. Reach forward with your dominant hand and foot
3. Move your racket arm up, palm down, and racket parallel to the floor
4. Put your weight slightly on your front foot

a

EXECUTION

1. Pivot and reach in the direction of the shuttle
2. Place your racket under the dropping shuttle
3. Put your wrist in laid back, or cocked, position
4. Drop your racket down; lift to contact the shuttle
5. Apply shoulder lift to bump shuttle over the net

b

FOLLOW-THROUGH

1. Continue swing up with the shuttle's flight
2. Keep a firm wrist and lift from your shoulder
3. Push off with your feet back toward mid-court

c

Misstep

Your reaction and movement on the court are slow. As a result, you have a hard time getting to the shuttle on returns and sustaining the rally.

Correction

Spend more time on your training and conditioning. Get in better shape and practice your footwork.

Players at all levels of badminton competition experience problems in executing the drop shot. Practice and repetition will provide you with more success on the court.

Drop Shot Drill 1. *Underhand Drop Shot at Net*

Player A throws the shuttle with an overhand toss just over the net toward player B, who steps toward the net with his or her dominant foot and hits a forehand underhand hairpin drop shot. These forehand underhand drop shot returns should land between the short service line and the net (figure 5.5). Player G returns shuttles to player A. Players rotate after three attempts. Player A takes the place of player G, player B replaces player A, player G moves behind player F, and so on until all players have been at each position. Repeat with backhand underhand hairpin drop shots.

Success Check

- Lead with your dominant hand and arm.
- Lift from your shoulder.
- Bump shuttle over the net.

Score Your Success

Hit three good forehand underhand drop shots = 5 points

Hit two good forehand underhand drop shots = 3 points

Hit one good forehand underhand drop shot = 1 point

Your score ___

Hit three good backhand underhand drop shots = 5 points

Hit two good backhand underhand drop shots = 3 points

Hit one good backhand underhand drop shot = 1 point

Your score ___

Your total score ___

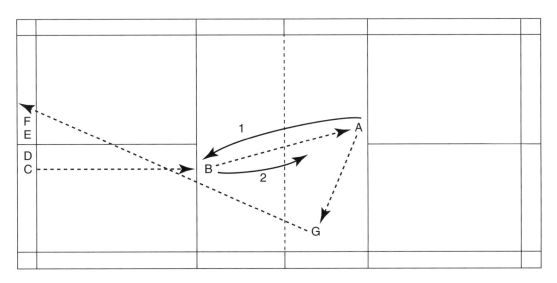

Figure 5.5 Underhand drop shot at net drill.

Drop Shot Drill 2. *Crosscourt Drop Shot at Net*

Player A throws the shuttle with an overhand toss just over the net toward player B, who steps toward the net with her dominant foot and hits an underhand crosscourt drop shot from her forehand or backhand side (figure 5.6). These underhand crosscourt drop shot returns should travel close to the top of the net and land between the short service line and the net. Player C retrieves shuttles and returns them to player A. Players rotate after three attempts until all players have been at each position.

Success Check

- Lead with your dominant hand and arm.
- Lift from the shoulder.
- Angle racket face crosscourt and push the shuttle over the net.

Score Your Success

Hit three good crosscourt drop shots = 5 points

Hit two good crosscourt drop shots = 3 points

Hit one good crosscourt drop shot = 1 point

Your score ___

Figure 5.6   Crosscourt drop shot at net.

Drop Shot Drill 3. *Tumble Drop Shot at Net*

Player A throws the shuttle with an overhand toss just over the net toward player B, who steps toward the net with his or her dominant foot and hits an underhand tumble drop shot from his or her forehand or backhand side (figure 5.7). Player C tallies the shots and returns shuttles to player A. When taking your turn as player B, keep your racket face parallel to the floor and push under the dropping shuttle so it will flip upside down as it makes contact and tumble as it falls. These tumble drop shot returns should fall close to the net and land well inside the short service line. Players rotate after three attempts until all players have been at each position.

Success Check

- Lift from your shoulder.
- Brush shuttle with a sideways motion of your wrist.
- Slice shuttle on contact with racket face causing a tumbling action.

Score Your Success

Hit three good tumble drop shots = 5 points

Hit two good tumble drop shots = 3 points

Hit one good tumble drop shot = 1 point

Your score ___

Figure 5.7 Tumble drop shot at net drill.

Drop Shot Drill 4. *Hairpin Drop Shot at Net*

In this drill, one partner begins the rally by hitting an underhand drop shot to his or her partner (figure 5.8). The drop shot should be aimed inside of the short service line. The rally continues until one partner misses the return. Players must hit only drop shots. This little game can be simply a rally drill or you may keep score. When one partner misses, the other partner gets a point. You may play games to 11 or 15 points. It does not matter which partner begins the rally. Either partner may score.

Success Check

- Allow racket head to lead.
- Contact shuttle in front of the body.
- Allow racket to block shuttle just over net.

Score Your Success

If you play this drill as simply a rally drill:

Rally for at least 5 minutes without a miss = 10 points

Rally for 3 to 4 minutes without a miss = 5 points

Rally for 1 to 2 minutes without a miss = 1 point

Your score ___

If you score the drill:

Win the game = 10 points

Lose the game = 5 points

Your score ___

Figure 5.8 Hairpin drop shot at the net drill.

Drop Shot Drill 5. *Self Toss-Overhead Drop Shot Return*

Because this drill is not a rally, begin with five or six shuttles. Stand sideways near the backcourt. Place a shuttle on your racket face, with your racket hand held palm up. Toss the shuttle upward with a lifting motion, placing the shuttle overhead for either a forehand or a backhand overhead stroke. After the shuttle leaves your racket, quickly lift your arm from the shoulder, placing your racket head downward at the end of your backswing. Extend your racket arm upward, leading with your elbow. Vigorously rotate your forearm and wrist, propelling the racket up to meet the shuttle at the highest possible point of contact. Shift your weight from your back foot to your front foot. Your racket face should contact the shuttle at a downward angle, with your racket leading the hand before contacting the shuttle. Good returns land near or inside the doubles short service line in the frontcourt. Execute 20 forehand returns and 20 backhand returns, gathering the shuttles when necessary.

To Increase Difficulty

- Recover to the ready position after each attempt.
- Alternate hitting forehand and backhand shots.
- Move toward the net and touch the short service line after each attempt and then recover to the backcourt.
- Use a tennis racket instead of your badminton racket. The increased weight provides more of an overload.

To Decrease Difficulty

- Have your body already turned in a sideways hitting stance.
- Begin with the racket already pointing upward.
- Begin with the weight already shifted to the front foot.

Success Check

- Point elbow upward with racket pointed downward.
- Allow hand to lead racket upward toward shuttle.
- Swing fast.

Score Your Success

Hit 20 good forehand drop shots = 5 points

Hit 15 to 19 good forehand drop shots = 3 points

Hit 10 to 14 good forehand drop shots = 1 point

Your score ____

Hit 20 good backhand drop shots = 5 points

Hit 15 to 19 good backhand drop shots = 3 points

Hit 10 to 14 good backhand drop shots = 1 point

Your score ____

Your total score ____

Drop Shot Drill 6. *Serve and Return Overhead Drop Shot*

Because this is not a rally drill, the setting partner begins with five or six shuttles. The setting partner sets up the other by hitting high, deep, friendly serves. (A friendly serve is directed to your partner and hit high enough so that he or she can return it easily.) The receiving partner returns each serve with either a forehand or backhand overhead drop shot return, down and just over the net. The partner setting up is near his or her short service line and the receiving partner is in the backcourt, near the doubles back service line. Good returns land between the net and the short service line on the setter's side of the court. The receiving partner executes 30 forehand and 30 backhand returns before the partners reverse roles.

Success Check

- Lead with the racket head.
- Angle shuttle downward.
- Block shuttle with your racket just over the net.

Score Your Success

Hit 30 good forehand overhead drop shots = 10 points

Hit 20 to 29 good forehand overhead drop shots = 5 points

Hit 10 to 19 good forehand overhead drop shots = 1 point

Your score ___

Hit 30 good backhand overhead drop shots = 10 points

Hit 20 to 29 good backhand overhead drop shots = 5 points

Hit 10 to 19 good backhand overhead drop shots = 1 point

Your score ___

Your total score ___

Drop Shot Drill 7. Drop Shot Three-Shot Rally

One partner begins the rally by setting up the other with a high, deep, friendly serve. The receiving partner returns the serve with a forehand or backhand overhead drop shot return down and just over the net. The setting partner is near his or her short service line and returns the receiving partner's drop shot with an underhand drop shot at the net. This is a three-shot rally so the setting partner begins with four or six shuttles. Good returns land between the net and the short service line on both sides of the court. This is a continuous drill. Execute 30 forehand returns and reverse roles. Execute 30 backhand returns.

Because the original server ends up returning the receiving partner's drop shot, another option is for players to alternate roles at the beginning of each rally. So player A serves to player B who hits a forehand overhead drop shot back to player A. Player A returns player B's drop shot with an underhand drop shot. Since player B ends up with the shuttle, player B serves for the next rally. Complete 30 forehand returns then repeat the drill, hitting backhand returns.

Success Check

- Allow racket head to lead.
- Extend your arm; contact the shuttle in front of your body.
- Angle the shuttle downward.

Score Your Success

Hit 30 good forehand drop shots = 10 points

Hit 20 to 29 good forehand drop shots = 5 points

Hit 10 to 19 good forehand drop shots = 1 point

Your score ___

Hit 30 good backhand drop shots = 10 points

Hit 20 to 29 good backhand drop shots = 5 points

Hit 10 to 19 good backhand drop shots = 1 point

Your score ___

Your total score ___

Drop Shot Drill 8. *Clear-Drop-Drop-Clear Continuous Rally*

One partner sets up the other by hitting a high, deep, friendly underhand clear. The receiving partner returns the serve with a forehand or backhand overhead drop shot return just over the net. The server then returns this drop shot with a hairpin drop shot. The receiving partner moves into the net and returns the hairpin drop shot with an underhand clear. The rally continues indefinitely in this clear-drop-drop-clear pattern. The partner who sets up needs to begin with one or two shuttles. This is a continuous drill in which the rally should continue as long as possible. Good returns need to land near or inside the short service line.

To Increase Difficulty

- Recover to ready position at centercourt after each attempt.
- Hit faster drop shots or alternate hitting crosscourt drop shots with straight-ahead drops.
- Require the hitter to wait in the centercourt position. Have your partner deliver a mixture of faster crosscourt drop shots that require you to move farther or more quickly to make an effective return.

To Decrease Difficulty

- Turn your body already sideways to the net in your hitting stance.
- Begin with your racket arm already held up and your racket angled slightly downward.
- Begin with your weight already shifted to your nondominant foot.

Success Check

- Use the correct grip and ready position.
- Allow your racket to block the shuttle close to the net.
- Attempt to make the rally last.

Score Your Success

Complete 30 clear-drop-drop-clears in one continuous rally = 10 points

Complete 20 to 29 clear-drop-drop-clears in one continuous rally = 5 points

Complete 10 to 19 clear-drop-drop-clears in one continuous rally = 1 point

Your score ____

Drop Shot Drill 9. *Diagonal Drop Shot Rally*

Player A begins the rally by clearing to player B's deep forehand or backhand side (figure 5.9). Player B hits a diagonal or crosscourt drop shot. Player A steps in slightly and blocks the return with a straight-ahead net drop shot. Player B redrops straight ahead to player A's side at the net. Player A crosscourt clears to player B's deep forehand or backhand side and the rally starts over. The sequence is clear: crosscourt drop shot, net drop, net drop, crosscourt clear. Players can hit all forehand drop shots, all backhand drop shots, or a mix. This is a continuous rally to work on diagonal speed or movement on the court.

To Increase Difficulty

- Include at random a crosscourt net drop shot instead of clearing out crosscourt at the end of the sequence.
- Hit the clear lower to give your partner less time.
- Hit the drop shot faster to give yourself less time.

To Decrease Difficulty

- Hit the clear higher to give your partner more time.

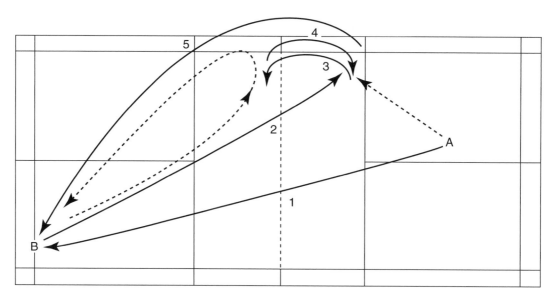

Figure 5.9 Diagonal drop shot rally.

- Hit the drop shot slower to give yourself more time.
- Split the drill into two drills, one a forehand drill only and the other a backhand drill only.

Success Check

- Contact the shuttle in front of your body by allowing the racket head to lead.
- Extend your racket arm to angle shuttle diagonally downward.
- Allow shuttle to travel just over the net.

Score Your Success

Complete five consecutive rallies = 10 points

Complete three or four consecutive rallies = 5 points

Complete one or two consecutive rallies = 1 point

Your score ___

SUCCESS SUMMARY OF THE DROP SHOT

Remember to prepare quickly. Pull your racket forward to make contact with the shuttle in front of your body. Swing your racket arm up with the racket head leading. Block the overhead drop shot with the racket face angled downward. Allow your hand and racket to follow through naturally. Complete the drop shot by pushing off and propelling yourself back to midcourt with your dominant foot.

Practice until the drop shot is a continuous, rhythmic motion that results in an effective, accurate, and deceptive stroke. Attempt to visualize each stroke and critique your thoughts out loud with a coach, instructor, or experienced player. Before you advance to the next step, record and tally your drill scores from this step.

Drop Shot Drills

1. Underhand Drop Shot at Net	___ out of 10
2. Crosscourt Drop Shot at Net	___ out of 5
3. Tumble Drop Shot at Net	___ out of 5
4. Hairpin Drop Shot at Net	___ out of 10
5. Self Toss-Overhead Drop Shot Return	___ out of 10
6. Serve and Return Overhead Drop Shot	___ out of 20
7. Drop Shot Three-Shot Rally	___ out of 20
8. Clear-Drop-Drop-Clear Continuous Rally	___ out of 10
9. Diagonal Drop Shot Rally	___ out of 10
Total	___ **out of 100**

If you scored at least 70 out of a possible 100 points, you are ready to move on to the next step. If you scored fewer than 70 points, repeat the drills that were difficult for you. Have a coach, instructor, or experienced player evaluate your skill.

Let's look ahead to step 6, the smash. The smash is usually a put-away of a short or shallow return. It is the shot of choice in doubles play. In badminton doubles, the objective is to get the offensive edge and keep it. Most returns in doubles should be directed down into your opponent's court. The smash is similar to the spike in volleyball. It kills or ends the rally and scores a point for the person or team winning the rally.

Smash

The smash is hit fast, downward with force, and steep, to put away any bird that has been hit up and short. The smash can be hit only from the overhead position. The shuttle is hit with power, but you should get your timing and balance before trying to get excessive speed on your smash. The most important characteristic of a good overhead smash besides speed is the downward angle. The bird is contacted farther in front of the body than the clear or the drop shot. Your racket face is angled to direct the bird more downward. If your angle is steep enough, the smash may be unreturnable.

Several characteristics of the smash also present problems for the player doing the smashing. If the smash is returned, you will have very little time to recover. The overhead smash requires a lot of energy and can quickly tire you out. Also, the farther you are from the net, the less steep your smash will be. Therefore, it is important for you to choose the correct opportunity to use your smash most effectively. The further you are from the net when you hit the smash, the more velocity the bird will lose as it travels to the opponent, thus making it easier to return.

The value of the overhead smash is that it gives your opponent very little time to prepare or return any shuttle that he or she hits up and short. The smash is used extensively in doubles. High-speed motion cinematography has shown that the overhead smash loses approximately two-thirds of its initial velocity by the time it reaches the opponent on the other side of the net. The steeper the angle you can create, the less time your opponent will have to react. Also, the more accurate your smash, the more court your opponent has to cover.

A smash that is not angled downward is generally less effective. The shuttle stays in the air longer and gives your opponent more time to potentially make a return. However, occasionally a hard flat smash can surprise an opponent who is crouched, ready to receive a steeply-angled smash, but is caught off-guard by an unintended high smash in which the shuttle reached the defender at shoulder height rather than below the waist. Because the defender is expecting a steep smash and his or her racket was low to the ground, he or she has little time to raise the racket to catch the shot, resulting in a miss-hit.

FOREHAND SMASH

The intention of the overhead forehand smash should be to suggest that an overhead clear or drop shot is about to be hit. The difference is primarily in racket speed. To execute a good forehand overhead smash, assume the handshake grip and move into waiting position behind and in line with the oncoming shuttle (figure 6.1a). As you move into position, pivot at your waist and turn your shoulders sideways to the net. Take your racket back and drop the racket head down behind your shoulder blades with your racket arm elbow pointing up.

Throw your racket up to meet the shuttle with your elbow leading. Take the overhead forehand smash as high as possible and in front of your body. Your racket head must move at a rapid rate as it goes out to meet the shuttle. Angle your racket face downward at contact (figure 6.1b). Keep your balance to achieve the maximum power from your shoulders, racket arm, and wrist. After contact, your forearm pronates rapidly with follow-through down and in line with the flight of the shuttle (figure 6.1c). Your racket head finishes pointing downward. As you complete your weight shift from back to front, your nondominant shoulder and arm assist in completing a vigorous upper-body rotation, and the scissoring action of your legs propels you back toward centercourt.

Figure 6.1   Forehand Smash

PREPARATION

1. Use the handshake grip
2. Recover into waiting or receiving stance
3. Turn your shoulders with feet up and back
4. Hold your racket arm up with racket head pointed up
5. Distribute your weight evenly on the balls of your feet

a

(continued)

Figure 6.1 *(continued)*

b

c

EXECUTION

1. Put your weight on your rear foot
2. Hold your nondominant arm out for balance
3. Place your wrist in a cocked position with your backswing
4. Swing forward and up to contact as high as possible
5. Throw your racket out and upward with your racket face down
6. Allow your nondominant arm to aid in speeding your upper-body rotation
7. Have your racket head follow the direction of the shuttle

FOLLOW-THROUGH

1. Swing down and across your body
2. Use scissoring action and push off with both feet
3. Use momentum of swing to return to centercourt

Misstep

Your arm swing and resulting smash are poorly timed. You slush, or miss-hit, the shuttle and hit a weak return.

Correction

Spend more time on your smash and practice your stroking action so you make contact at the correct time.

Misstep

You are off balance and unable to generate maximum speed and power on the smash and thus your smash is more easily returned.

Correction

Keep your nondominant arm extended for balance.

Even if the initial speed of your smash reaches 200 miles per hour or more, the shuttle loses speed quickly and angles down toward the floor after passing over the net. High-speed motion film analysis indicates that the shuttle loses approximately two-thirds of its initial speed before getting to the opponent.

The powerful stroking action of the smash is similar to the overhead smash in tennis and is intended to put away any short return by an opponent. You may push the shuttle past the net player and force the backcourt player to hit his or her return up, giving you or your partner an opportunity to smash. The smash is particularly effective in doubles play; it can cause some indecision as to which player should make the return. The sooner and higher you contact the shuttle, the faster and steeper your smash returns will be. Another motive for using the smash or half-smash in doubles is to set up your partner for a kill near the net. The smash is often hit from deep in the backcourt, not to win the point since it likely will be returned, but so your partner can get to the net for the kill.

BACKHAND SMASH

The backhand smash is an advanced skill that requires proper timing, a higher skill level, and good eye–hand coordination. The backhand smash is also discussed in step 8. The intention of the overhead backhand smash should be to suggest that an overhead clear or drop shot is about to be hit. The difference is primarily in racket speed. To execute a good overhead backhand smash, assume the backhand, thumb-up grip and move into waiting position behind and in line with the oncoming shuttle (figure 6.2a). As you move into position, pivot at your waist and turn with your back toward the net. Take your racket back and drop the racket head down with your forearm held parallel to the floor. The racket and thumb of your backhand grip are pointing down in this waiting position.

Misstep

Your backhand smash has little power.

Correction

Lack of power could be caused by an incorrect grip. Use the handshake, or pistol, grip for both the forehand and backhand smash. However, the thumb is up on the backhand. This thumb-up position adds leverage and generates more power.

Throw your racket up to meet the shuttle with your elbow leading. Take the overhead backhand smash as high as possible. Your racket head must be moving at a rapid rate as it goes out to meet the shuttle. Angle your racket face downward at contact (figure 6.2b). Keep your balance to achieve the maximum power from your shoulders, racket arm, and wrist. After contact, your forearm supinates rapidly with your follow-through down and in line with the flight of the shuttle (figure 6.2c). Your racket head finishes pointing downward. Vigorous upper-body rotation along with your weight shift from back to front propels you back toward centercourt. The backhand smash loses speed quickly and angles down toward the floor after passing over the net.

Figure 6.2 | Backhand Smash

a

b

c

PREPARATION

1. Apply backhand handshake grip, with thumb up
2. Recover into waiting or receiving stance
3. Turn shoulders with back toward the net
4. Hold racket arm up and parallel to the floor
5. Point racket head downward
6. Distribute weight evenly on balls of feet

EXECUTION

1. Initially put weight on rear foot
2. Hold nondominant arm out for balance
3. For backswing wrist in cocked position with thumb down
4. Forward swing as high as possible with racket leading
5. Throw racket out and upward with racket face down
6. Use nondominant arm to speed rotation of upper body
7. Allow the racket head to follow in the direction shuttle is traveling

FOLLOW-THROUGH

1. Swing in line with the flight of the shuttle
2. Have swing follow downward naturally
3. Use forearm and push off with rear foot
4. Use upper-body swing and weight shift to return to centercourt

Misstep

Your backhand smash is weak, closely resembling a flat backhand drive.

Correction

Poor preparation leads to a weak backhand smash. Move quickly to get into proper hitting position. Turn your shoulders with both arms up. Assume the correct backhand grip, which allows for rapid supination.

The powerful stroking action of the backhand smash is intended to put away any short return or to force the opponent to hit returns up. In doubles play, a backhand smash may also create some indecision as to which player should make the return. The sooner and higher you contact the shuttle, the faster and steeper your smash returns will be.

Beginners and intermediate players often demonstrate incorrect technique and poor stroke production in executing the smash. Beginners and intermediate badminton players may not have developed the necessary eye–hand coordination to execute the backhand smash effectively. Practice and repetition will provide you with better timing, balance, and success when executing the overhead smash.

Smash Drill 1. *Shadow Smash*

Practice the forehand or backhand overhand smash motion with the racket cover on your racket. The added weight and air resistance aid in developing strength and endurance in your hitting arm.

Success Check

- Hold your nondominant arm up for balance.
- Cock your wrist with your elbow up, your racket back and down in backswing position.
- Lead with your wrist and hand, your racket trailing on the upward swing.

Score Your Success

Complete 30 forehand smash swings = 5 points

Complete 30 backhand smash swings = 5 points

Your score ___

Smash Drill 2. *Self-Toss and Smash Return*

Because this drill is not a rally, begin with five or six shuttles. Your partner should also start with five or six shuttles. Both you and your partner stand on opposite sides of the net near midcourt approximately 3 to 4 feet (about 1 meter) in front of the doubles back service line. Hold your racket, palm up, and place a shuttle on your racket face. Toss the shuttle up with an underhand lift, placing the shuttle in front of the dominant shoulder, slightly in front of your body. Swing your racket up with a forehand or backhand overhead strok-

ing motion, resulting in a smash return down at your partner's feet. A good return lands near your partner's feet at midcourt. You and your partner hit smashes simultaneously. Hit 30 forehand smashes and 30 backhand smashes.

Success Check

- Lead with the racket head.
- Angle the shuttle downward.
- Allow the racket to snap through.

Score Your Success

Hit 30 good forehand smashes = 10 points

Hit 20 to 29 good forehand smashes = 5 points

Hit 10 to 19 good forehand smashes = 1 point

Your score ___

Hit 30 good backhand smashes = 10 points

Hit 20 to 29 good backhand smashes = 5 points

Hit 10 to 19 good backhand smashes = 1 point

Your score ___

Your total score ___

Smash Drill 3. *Serve and Return Smash*

The partner who is setting up the other player begins with five or six shuttles because this is not a rally. Both partners are situated on opposite sides of the net near midcourt approximately 3 to 4 feet (about 1 m) in front of the doubles back service line. One partner sets up the other by hitting high, deep, friendly underhand serves. The receiving partner returns each serve with either a forehand or backhand overhead stroking motion resulting in a smash return at his or her partner's feet (figure 6.3). Good returns land near the set-

ting partner's feet at midcourt. The setting partner makes no attempt to return the smash. This is a repetitive drill in which the receiving partner executes 30 forehand and 30 backhand returns before the partners reverse roles.

Success Check

- Lead with the racket head.
- Contact the shuttle in front of your body.
- Angle the shuttle downward.

Figure 6.3 Serve and return smash drill.

Score Your Success

Hit 30 good forehand smashes = 10 points

Hit 20 to 29 good forehand smashes = 5 points

Hit 10 to 19 good forehand smashes = 1 point

Your score ___

Hit 30 good backhand smashes = 10 points

Hit 20 to 29 good backhand smashes = 5 points

Hit 10 to 19 good backhand smashes = 1 point

Your score ___

Your total score ___

Smash Drill 4. *Serve-Smash-Block Return*

This drill is a three-shot rally so the setting partner needs to begin with one or two shuttles. The setting partner begins the rally by setting up the other with a high, deep, friendly serve. The receiving partner returns the serve with a forehand or backhand overhead smash to his or her partner's feet. The setting partner is near his or her mid-court at the centerline and returns the receiving partner's smash with a blocked or underhand drop shot at the net. In this continuous drill, each partner should execute at least 30 serve-smash-drop shot rallies before the partners reverse roles. Good smash returns need to be angled down at the partner's feet. Good blocked drop shot returns should land between the net and the short service line on the court.

Success Check

- Lead with the racket head.
- Extend your arm.
- Block the shuttle with your racket just over the net on the smash return.

Score Your Success

Complete 30 good forehand rallies = 10 points

Complete 20 to 29 good forehand rallies = 5 points

Complete 10 to 19 good forehand rallies = 1 point

Your score ___

Complete 30 good backhand rallies = 10 points

Complete 20 to 29 good backhand rallies = 5 points

Complete 10 to 19 good backhand rallies = 1 point

Your score ___

Your total score ___

Smash Drill 5. *Clear-Smash-Drop-Clear Continuous Rally*

The setting partner (player A) begins with one or two shuttles. The setting partner sets up the other by hitting a high, deep, friendly underhand clear (figure 6.4). The receiving partner (player B) returns the serve with a forehand or backhand overhead smash return at the serving partner's feet. The server then returns the smash with a blocked drop shot return. The receiving partner moves into the net and returns the drop shot with an underhand clear. Player B should move into the net to return the drop shot (shot 3) with an underhand clear (shot 4). The rally continues indefinitely in this clear-smash-drop-clear pattern. Good drop shot returns land near or inside the short service line. Continue the rally as long as possible.

To Increase Difficulty

- Recover to ready position at centercourt after each attempt.

- Hit faster smashes or alternate hitting crosscourt drop shots with straight-ahead drops.

- Touch the net before returning to center-court.

- Have your partner deliver tighter drop shots closer to the net so you have to move farther or more quickly to make an effective return.

- Have your partner deliver a mixture of cross-court drop shots that require you to move farther or more quickly to make an effective return.

To Decrease Difficulty

- Turn your body already sideways to the net in your hitting stance.

- Begin with your racket arm already held up and racket angled slightly downward.

- Begin with your weight already shifted to your left foot.

- Have your partner deliver drop shot returns farther from the net so you can move less or more slowly to make an effective return.

- Make drop shot returns higher in order to give your partner more time.

Success Check

- Angle the smash down at your partner's feet.

- Block the shuttle with your racket close to the net on the return of the smash.

- Keep the rally going as long as possible.

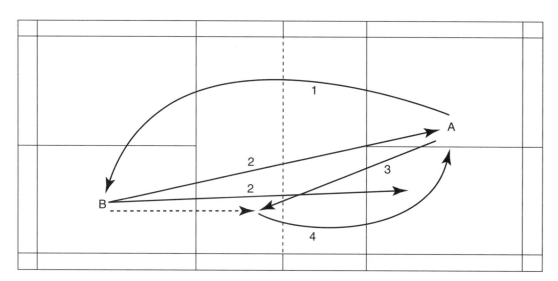

Figure 6.4 Clear-smash-drop-clear continuous rally.

Rally for at least 5 minutes without a miss = 10 points

Rally for 3 to 4 minutes without a miss = 5 points

Rally for 1 to 2 minutes without a miss = 1 point

Your score ___

Smash Drill 6.   *Smash Return Down the Line*

The setting partner begins with five or six shuttles because this is not a rally drill. Both players begin on opposite sides of the net near midcourt, approximately 3 to 4 feet (about 1 m) in front of the doubles back service line. The setting partner sets up the other by hitting high, deep, friendly underhand serves. The receiving partner returns each serve with a smash return down either sideline. Good returns land near either sideline at midcourt. The setting partner makes no attempt to return the smash. This is a repetitive drill. The receiving partner executes 30 smash returns down the sidelines before partners reverse roles.

Success Check

- Extend your arm.
- Contact the shuttle in front of your body on your nondominant side.
- Angle the shuttle downward.

Score Your Success

Hit 30 good smashes = 10 points

Hit 20 to 29 good smashes = 5 points

Hit 10 to 19 good smashes = 1 point

Your score ___

Smash Drill 7.   *Diagonal Forehand Smash Rally*

Player A begins the rally by clearing to player B's deep forehand or backhand side (figure 6.5). Player B hits a diagonal or crosscourt smash. Player A steps in slightly and blocks the return with a straight-ahead net drop shot. Player B redrops straight ahead to Player A's side at the net. Player A crosscourt clears to Player B's deep, forehand or backhand side and the rally starts

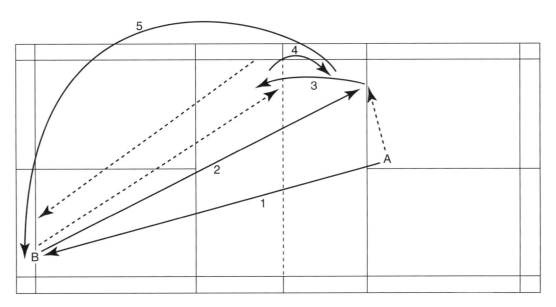

Figure 6.5   Diagonal forehand smash rally.

over. The sequence is clear, crosscourt smash, drop, drop, crosscourt clear. This is a continuous rally to work on diagonal speed or movement on the court.

To Increase Difficulty

- Recover to ready position at centercourt after each attempt.
- Hit faster diagonal smashes.
- Have your partner deliver tighter drop shots closer to the net so you have to move farther or more quickly to make an effective return.
- Include at random a crosscourt net drop shot instead of clearing out crosscourt at the end of the sequence. This mixture of crosscourt drop shots will require you to move farther or more quickly to make an effective return.

Success Check

- Angle smash down at partner's feet.
- Block the shuttle with the racket close to the net on the return of the smash.
- Make the rally last as long as possible.

Score Your Success

Rally for at least 5 minutes without a miss = 10 points

Rally for 3 to 4 minutes without a miss = 5 points

Rally for 1 to 2 minutes without a miss = 1 point

Your score ___

SUCCESS SUMMARY OF THE SMASH

Remember to prepare quickly. Swing your racket forward to make contact with the shuttle in front of your body. Swing your racket arm up with the racket head leading. Hit the overhead smash powerfully with the racket face angled downward. Allow your hand and racket to follow through naturally. Complete the smash by pushing off and propelling yourself back to midcourt with your dominant foot.

Practice until the overhead smash is a continuous, rhythmic motion that results in an effective, accurate, and powerful stroke. Visualize each overhead smash and critique your thoughts with an instructor, coach, or experienced player. Before you advance to the next step, record and tally your drill scores from this step.

Smash Drills	
1. Smash Shadow	___ out of 10
2. Self-Toss and Smash Return	___ out of 20
3. Serve and Return Smash	___ out of 20
4. Serve-Smash-Block Return	___ out of 20
5. Clear-Smash-Drop-Clear Continuous Rally	___ out of 10
6. Smash Return Down the Line	___ out of 10
7. Diagonal Forehand Smash Rally	___ out of 10
Total	___ *out of 100*

If you scored at least 75 out of a possible 100 points, you are ready to move on to the next step. If you scored fewer than 75 points, repeat the drills that were difficult for you. Have a coach, instructor, or experienced player evaluate your skill.

Step 7 discusses the drive. The drive travels in a flat trajectory over the net and parallel to the floor. The drive may be executed at various speeds, giving your opponent a different look with each changing speed. Some midcourt drives drop from lack of speed and only carry to half-court. Other drives may be hit with the same force as a smash and carry to backcourt quickly. The drive in doubles play is often used to entice the opposing team to return the push or midcourt drive with a clear, thus giving your team the offensive position.

Drive

The drive is a flat shot that directs the bird in a horizontal trajectory across the net. Both forehand and backhand drives send the shuttle just high enough to clear the net in a level or slightly downward path. The stroking action is similar to a sidearm throwing motion and usually is played down the sidelines of the court. The forehand and backhand drives provide a chance to work on footwork because the stroke is generally executed between shoulder and knee height to the left or right of centercourt. Therefore, it emphasizes reaching for the shuttle by shuffling or sliding the feet into position.

In singles and doubles, the drive is a safe, conservative return that will keep your opponents honest and require them to lift their returns. If you hit your drive with less power, your return resembles more of a push shot or midcourt drive.

The primary objective of the drive during play is to get the shuttle over the net quickly and, with the assistance of gravity, headed for the floor. Hit it away from your opponent to force him or her to move quickly. By getting the bird below net height, you will give your opponent less time and his or her return will necessarily be directed upward. If you perform the drive accurately and effectively, your opponent will need to hurry to make the returns and will become more fatigued, as well. A flatter, faster drive may be useful in getting the shuttle behind your opponent and potentially cause him or her to hit a weak return. Another option is to hit the drive into the opponent's body, making a return more difficult. This shot gives the opponent very little time to react and may in effect handcuff him or her and force a weak return or no return at all.

You may play all drives diagonally crosscourt or straight ahead down the sidelines. If you hit the drive below knee height with more power, the shuttle will be rising as it goes over the net and will continue to travel up into your opponent's court, giving your opponent the advantage. A slower-paced midcourt drive that reaches its peak at the net and descends from there is particularly valuable in doubles when you do not want to hit the bird up to your opponent.

FOREHAND DRIVE

When the shuttle is returned between shoulder and knee height to the forehand side of your centercourt position, the forehand drive becomes one of your return options. From the ready position, you will need to reach for the shuttle with your dominant arm and leg in order to hit a low return to your forehand. If you are hitting a drive return, pivot on your nondominant foot and turn your shoulders as you reach to your side with your dominant arm and leg. Draw your racket arm back in a sidearm, backswing motion by flexing your elbow and cocking your wrist (figure 7.1a). The backswing and handshake grip place the racket parallel to the floor with your palm up.

As you swing your racket arm forward, put your body weight on your dominant foot. Your racket arm extends, rolls your forearm over, and contacts the shuttle as the wrist uncocks (figure 7.1b). Your racket foot should be pointing toward the sideline. Flex your racket leg to extend and push off back toward centercourt. Strike the shuttle in front of your racket foot at the highest possible point and well away from your body so your swing is not restricted. Elbow extension, forearm rotation, and wrist action provide the proper sequence of action.

Misstep

You lack full arm extension at contact and make contact with the shuttle too close to your body.

Correction

Make contact well away from the body so your swing is not restricted.

Your hand and wrist allow your racket arm to follow through naturally. Rapid forearm pronation provides most of the power. The racket travels through the contact area and then forward in the direction of the flight of the shuttle (figure

7.1c). Your forearm continues to pronate on the forehand drive and finishes palm down. At or soon after contact, transfer your body weight rapidly as your racket leg and foot push your body back toward midcourt.

Figure 7.1   Forehand Drive

PREPARATION

1. Apply handshake grip
2. Recover into waiting or receiving stance
3. Hold racket arm up and in front of your chest
4. Distribute your weight evenly over both feet

a

(continued)

Figure 7.1 (continued)

b

c

EXECUTION

1. Reach with your dominant foot
2. Pivot and turn in the direction of the oncoming shuttle
3. Place wrist in cocked position, palm up with backswing
4. Swing forward led by your elbow
5. Contact shuttle as high as possible
6. Provide power through forearm supination
7. Use your hand and wrist roll over

FOLLOW-THROUGH

1. Continue to swing upward in line with shuttle flight
2. Swing naturally toward the net
3. Finish with your palm down
4. Push off with your foot
5. Use momentum of swing to return to centercourt

Misstep

You lack pace on your returns.

Correction

Lead with your elbow bent and your forearm parallel to the floor. Extend your arm and snap the racket through.

BACKHAND DRIVE

When the shuttle is returned between shoulder and knee height to the backhand side of your centercourt position, the backhand drive becomes one of your return options. To hit a low return on the backhand side, you will need to pivot and execute a crossover step, reaching for the shuttle with your dominant arm and leg. Begin in ready position and hold the racket with a backhand handshake grip. If you are hitting a backhand drive return, pivot on your nondominant foot and turn your shoulders as you reach to your backhand side with your dominant arm and leg. Draw your racket arm behind your body by flexing your elbow and cocking your wrist. Your backswing and backhand grip place the racket parallel to the floor with your palm down (figure 7.2a).

Misstep

You do not meet the oncoming shuttle with a flat racket face.

Correction

Often an incorrect grip causes this error. Use the handshake, or pistol, grip. Keep thumb up on the backhand. As you reach for the oncoming shuttle, vigorous forearm rotation provides most of the needed power to execute the drive effectively.

As your racket arm swings forward, transfer your body weight to your dominant foot. Point this racket foot toward the sideline. Flex your racket leg to enable you to push off toward centercourt. Extend your racket arm, roll your forearm over, and contact the shuttle as the wrist uncocks (figure 7.2b). Strike the shuttle in front of your racket foot at the highest possible point and well away from your body so your swing is not restricted. Elbow extension, forearm rotation, and wrist action provide the proper sequence of action.

Your hand and wrist allow your racket arm to follow through naturally. Rapid forearm supination provides most of the power. Your racket travels through the contact area and then forward in the direction of the flight of the shuttle (figure 7.2c). Your forearm continues to supinate on your backhand drive and finishes palm up. At or soon after contact, transfer your body weight rapidly as your racket leg and foot push your body back toward midcourt.

Figure 7.2   Backhand Drive

PREPARATION

1. Apply handshake backhand, thumb-up grip
2. Recover into waiting or receiving stance
3. Hold your racket arm up and in front of your chest
4. Distribute your weight evenly on both feet

a   *(continued)*

Figure 7.2 (continued)

b

c

EXECUTION

1. Reach with your dominant foot
2. Pivot and turn in the direction of the on-coming shuttle
3. Flex your dominant elbow
4. Place your wrist in cocked position, palm down with your backswing
5. Lead forward swing by your elbow
6. Contact shuttle as high as possible
7. Provide power with forearm supination
8. Use hand and wrist roll over

FOLLOW-THROUGH

1. Continue swing upward in line with shuttle flight
2. Swing naturally toward net
3. Finish with your palm up
4. Push off with your foot
5. Use the momentum of your swing to return to centercourt

Misstep

You sometimes hit drives with too much wrist flexion. The term *wrist snap* is a misnomer; *forearm rotation* is more correct.

Correction

Move quickly to get into the proper hitting position and make contact at the proper time. Your technique and timing can be improved with concentration and practice.

Common faults are apparent at all levels of badminton play. Repetition and practice will assist you in developing good stroke production in the drive shot for more success in badminton.

Drive Drill 1. *Shadow Drive*

Practice the forehand and backhand drive swinging motions with the racket cover on your racket. The added weight and air resistance aid in developing strength and endurance in your hitting arm. Make your racket swish. Execute 30 forehand shadow swings and 30 backhand shadow swings.

Success Check

- Execute the drive sidearm swinging motion.
- Put your wrist in cocked, or in laid back, position on your backswing.

- Lead with your elbow, racket trailing on the forward swing.
- Finish palm down on your forehand and palm up on your backhand.

Score Your Success

Complete 30 forehand drive swings = 5 points

Complete 30 backhand drive swings = 5 points

Your score ___

Drive Drill 2. *Push or Drive Return From Midcourt*

Player A tosses or hits the shuttle near midcourt toward player B, who steps toward the sideline with his or her dominant foot and hits a sidearm push or drive shot from his or her forehand side (figure 7.3). These push or drive shot returns should land near midcourt between the back boundary line and the net. Player C returns the shuttles to player A. Players rotate after three attempts until all players have been at each position. Repeat drill on the backhand side.

Success Check

- Lead with your dominant foot and elbow.
- Extend the racket arm from the elbow.
- Push the shuttle over the net down the sideline near midcourt.

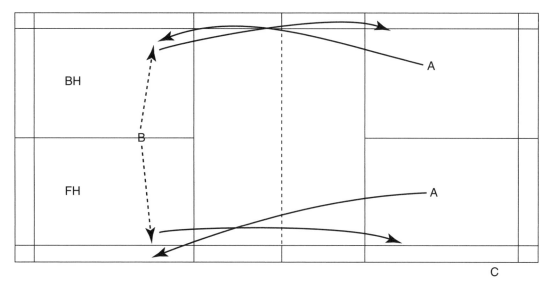

Figure 7.3 Push or drive return from midcourt.

Score Your Success

Hit three good forehand drives = 5 points

Hit two good forehand drives = 3 points

Hit one good forehand drive = 1 point

Your score ___

Hit three good backhand drives = 5 points

Hit two good backhand drives = 3 points

Hit one good backhand drive = 1 point

Your score ___

Your total score ___

Drive Drill 3. *Crosscourt Drive Shot at Net*

Player A throws the shuttle with an overhand toss near midcourt toward player B, who steps toward the sideline with his or her dominant foot and hits a diagonal, crosscourt push or drive shot from his or her forehand side. These sidearm, crosscourt push or drive returns should travel close to the top of the net and land between the short service line and the back boundary line near midcourt. Player G should return the shuttles to player A. Players rotate after three attempts. Player A takes the place of player G, player B replaces player A, and player G moves behind player F, and so on until all players have been at each position. Repeat the drill, hitting from the backhand side.

Success Check

- Lead with your dominant leg and arm.
- Extend from your elbow, allowing forearm rotation.
- Angle your racket face crosscourt and push, or drive, the shuttle in a flat path toward midcourt.

Score Your Success

Hit three good forehand drive shots = 5 points

Hit two good forehand drive shots = 3 points

Hit one good forehand drive shot = 1 point

Your score ___

Hit three good backhand drive shots = 5 points

Hit two good backhand drive shots = 3 points

Hit one good backhand drive shot = 1 point

Your score ___

Your total score ___

Drive Drill 4. *Toss and Hit Drive*

Because this drill is not a rally, begin with five or six shuttles. Set yourself up by tossing a shuttle to your forehand or backhand side. Hit a drive return. A good drive return will land near or beyond your partner's position on the other side of the net. Execute 20 forehand drive returns and 20 backhand drive returns as your partner does the same from the opposite side of the net.

Success Check

- Push off and reach with your dominant hand and foot.
- Snap the racket through the contact area with forearm pronation.
- Finish with your hand palm down on forehand and palm up on backhand.
- Hit flat and quick.

Score Your Success

Hit 20 good forehand drives = 5 points
Hit 15 to 19 good forehand drives = 3 points
Hit 10 to 14 good forehand drives = 1 point
Your score ___

Hit 20 good backhand drives = 5 points
Hit 15 to 19 good backhand drives = 3 points
Hit 10 to 14 good backhand drives = 1 point
Your score ___
Your total score ___

Drive Drill 5. *Return With Drive*

The partner setting up the other needs to begin with five or six shuttles because this is not a rally drill. One partner sets up the other by hitting flat, friendly, midcourt drives. The receiving partner returns each drive with either a forehand or backhand drive. Good returns land near or beyond the setting-up partner's position at midcourt. This is a repetitive drill in which the receiving partner should execute at least 30 returns before the partners reverse roles.

Success Check

- Lead with your elbow, palm up initially.
- Pronate your forearm, finish palm down.
- Hit flat and sidearm.

Score Your Success

Hit 30 good drives = 10 points
Hit 20 to 29 good drives = 5 points
Hit 10 to 19 good drives = 1 point
Your score ___

Drive Drill 6. *Drive Four-Way Rally*

This rally begins with four players on a court. Partners face each other on opposite sides of the net. Partner A sets up partner B by pushing or driving a flat, friendly, midcourt forehand drive down the line. Partner B returns the drive with a backhand drive to partner A. Partner C sets up partner D by pushing or driving a flat, friendly, midcourt forehand drive down the line. Partner D returns the drive with a backhand drive to partner C. These are rallies so each partner needs to begin with only one or two shuttles. It is a continuous drill in which all partners should attempt to execute as many drive returns as possible, keeping the rally going indefinitely. Returns should be flat and near enough to the partner to allow the rally to continue. Good returns should be sent directly back at the partner near midcourt.

To Increase Difficulty

- Use only one shuttle between all four players and increase the pace to develop defensive skills and racket control. Faster, flatter drives angled both straight-ahead and crosscourt place emphasis on ready position and ability to react.

- Recover to ready position after each attempt.

- Shuffle sideways and touch the centerline between drives, and then return to ready position.

- Hit drives with a faster, flatter trajectory. Hit this quick, flat drive slightly sooner and more in front of you. This flat-flat-flat exchange may be so fast that you do not have time to step, but only to turn your hips and maneuver the racket quickly from forehand to backhand depending on your partner's pace and direction.

To Decrease Difficulty

- Play only a two-shot rally, emphasizing racket control and control of the direction of the drive return.

- Turn your body already in the sideways hitting stance for either forehand or backhand drives from midcourt.

- Begin with your racket arm already held in backswing position before attempting the forehand or backhand drive.

- Begin with your weight already shifted to your dominant leg and foot and with your racket arm already in backswing position.

Success Check

- Lead with your elbow.
- Swing fast and execute quick flat-flat exchanges.
- Direct return toward your partner's body.

Score Your Success

Rally for at least 5 minutes without a miss = 10 points

Rally for 3 to 4 minutes without a miss = 5 points

Rally for 1 to 2 minutes without a miss = 1 point

Your score ____

Drive Drill 7. *Continuous Drive Rally*

This is a rally so the partner starting needs to begin with only one or two shuttles. One partner sets up the other by pushing or driving a flat, friendly, midcourt drive. The receiving partner returns the drive with a forehand or backhand drive to his or her partner (figure 7.4). This is a continuous drill in which both partners should attempt to execute as many drive returns as possible, keeping the rally going indefinitely. Returns should be flat and near enough to the partner to allow the rally to continue. Good returns should be sent directly back at the partner near midcourt.

To Increase Difficulty

- Recover to ready position after each attempt.
- Alternate hitting forehand and backhand overhead drives.
- Shuffle sideways and touch the singles sideline between drives and then return to ready position.
- Hit drives with a faster, flatter trajectory. Hit this quick, flat drive slightly sooner and more in front of you. This flat-flat-flat exchange may be so fast that you do not have time to step, but only to turn your hips and maneuver the racket quickly from forehand to backhand depending on your partner's pace and direction.

To Decrease Difficulty

- Have your body already turned in sideways hitting stance for either forehand or backhand drives from midcourt.
- Begin with your racket arm already held in backswing position before attempting the forehand or backhand drive.
- Begin with your weight already shifted to your dominant leg and foot and with your racket arm already in backswing position.

Success Check

- Lead with your elbow.
- Swing fast and execute quick flat-flat exchanges.
- Direct return toward partner's body.

Score Your Success

Rally for at least 5 minutes without a miss = 10 points

Rally for 3 to 4 minutes without a miss = 5 points

Rally for 1 to 2 minutes without a miss = 1 point

Your score ____

Figure 7.4 Continuous drive rally drill.

Drive Drill 8. *Alternate Sideline and Crosscourt Drives*

This is a rally so the partner starting the rally needs to begin with only one or two shuttles. Player A will hit only down-the-line drive shot returns and player B will hit only crosscourt drive shot returns. Player A begins by pushing or driving a flat, friendly, midcourt drive down the sideline to player B's backhand. Player B returns the drive with a crosscourt drive to player A's backhand side (figure 7.5). Player A then pushes or drives his or her return down the sideline. Player B then hits a forehand drive crosscourt. This is a continuous drill in which both partners should attempt to execute as many drive returns as possible, keeping the rally going indefinitely. Returns should be flat and near enough to the partner to allow the rally to continue. Good returns should be sent either down the sideline or crosscourt near midcourt. Each rally should go for as long as possible. When the rally ends, change the sequence to allow player A to hit crosscourt and player B to hit down the sideline.

Success Check

- Lead arm extension with elbow followed by forearm rotation.
- Swing under control, pushing or directing the shuttle to midcourt.
- Hit flat crosscourt and down-the-sideline exchanges.

Score Your Success

Rally for at least 5 minutes without a miss = 10 points

Rally for 3 to 4 minutes without a miss = 5 points

Rally for 1 to 2 minutes without a miss = 1 point

Your score ___

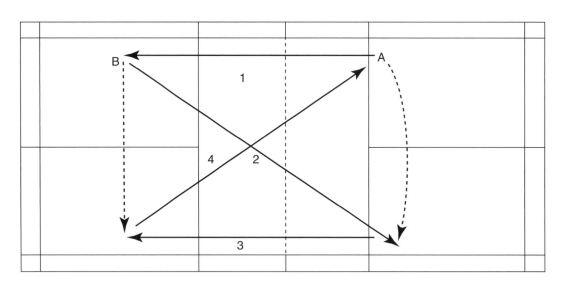

Figure 7.5 Alternate sidelines and crosscourt drives.

SUCCESS SUMMARY OF THE DRIVE

As you prepare to be observed and evaluated on your forehand and backhand drives, use the correct grips and prepare quickly. Make contact with the shuttle out to your side as soon as possible in front of your dominant foot or leg. Your footwork for these strokes requires a rapid shuffle and reach, followed by a quick change of direction back to midcourt. Swing your racket arm out and lead with your elbow as you swing your arm in a sidearm throwing motion. Allow your hand and racket to follow through naturally. Emphasize vigorous forearm rotation, finishing palm down on the forehand drive and palm up on the backhand drive. Complete the stroke by pushing off and propelling yourself back to midcourt with your dominant foot.

Practice the forehand and backhand drives until you have a fast, whip-like motion that results in an effective and accurate stroke. Attempt to visualize each stroke and discuss your thoughts out loud with an instructor, coach, or experienced player. Before you advance to the next step, record and tally your drill scores from this step.

Drive Drills

1. Shadow Drive	___ out of 10
2. Push or Drive Return From Midcourt	___ out of 10
3. Crosscourt Drive Shot at Net	___ out of 10
4. Toss and Hit Drive	___ out of 10
5. Return With Drive	___ out of 10
6. Drive Four-Way Rally	___ out of 10
7. Continuous Drive Rally	___ out of 10
8. Alternate Sideline and Crosscourt Drives	___ out of 10
Total	___ **out of 80**

If you scored at least 60 out of a possible 80 points, you are ready to move on to the next step. If you scored fewer than 60 points, repeat the drills that were difficult for you. Have a coach, instructor, or experienced player evaluate your skill.

Step 8 introduces and describes advanced techniques. These include more advanced overhead strokes, higher skill development in net play, serve and returns of serve needed to play at a more advanced level, and deception in stroke making and stroke production. This step is designed to build on the basic skills fundamentals and to help the player advance beyond beginner to become a competitive badminton player.

Advanced Techniques

Advanced techniques include skills and drills beyond those of the beginning player. These techniques are designed for the athlete who wishes to play at the elite level. They require a higher level of athletic ability and training. The following advanced skills are presented in a five-part format of overhead strokes, net play, serve and return of serve, deception, and trick shots.

Beginning and intermediate players must master the basic skills and fundamentals before they are ready to pursue these more advanced skills and techniques. However, even players who may not have the experience or practice to execute these higher levels of expertise may still enjoy trying them anyway just for fun or practice. These more advanced skills and techniques will be needed for competitive players but recreational players may never use them extensively. Players who plan to advance to the elite level will benefit from this step, but those who wish to play only at a recreational level may choose to skip this step.

OVERHEAD STROKES

Stroke production is the ability to reproduce a sequence of returns in random order with consistency and control. The preparation for hitting all overhead strokes begins with a sideways hitting stance with the nondominant leg forward and the dominant leg back (figure 8.1a).

All overhead strokes should look the same. Several events happen almost simultaneously during the overhead stroke: the weight shifts forward from the dominant foot to the nondominant foot, the upper body rotates, the back arches, and the arm extends (figure 8.1b). The anterior muscles of the front side of the body are stretched; the back is arched. The trunk rotates vigorously and the racket arm is thrown upward (extended) to meet the oncoming shuttle. The legs extend, propelling the body upward, and they execute a scissoring action to assist the shoulder rotation. The dominant leg and upper body both swing forward, providing additional power. If the stroke is made with the body in the air, this scissoring action causes the dominant leg to swing forward with the nondominant leg swinging backward and absorbing most of the landing force.

The follow-through (figure 8.1c) is downward and in line with the flight of the shuttle. The forearm pronates with the hand and wrist allowing the racket to follow through naturally. The racket hand finishes with the palm facing outward or away from the body.

Figure 8.1   Overhead Stroke

a   *b*   *c*

PREPARATION

1. Stand in the sideways hitting stance
2. Place your nondominant leg forward, your dominant leg back

EXECUTION

1. Shift your weight
2. Rotate your upper body
3. Arch your back
4. Meet the shuttle by extending your arm
5. Scissor your legs

FOLLOW-THROUGH

1. Stand in the sideways hitting stance
2. Throw your racket up to meet the oncoming shuttle in front of your dominant shoulder
3. Place your racket face out to meet the shuttle with your hand leading and hitting the shuttle in an upward trajectory
4. Allow your racket to follow the path of the shuttle with vigorous upper-body rotation
5. Shift your body weight from back to front, transferring your weight from your dominant foot to your nondominant foot
6. Generate the majority of the force you need with forearm rotation, or pronation
7. Allow your hand and wrist to slow down your racket and arm
8. Allow the palm of your dominant hand to finish outward away from your body

Misstep

The overhead stroke lacks power or the shuttle loses power as it goes over the net.

Correction

A lack of power in the overhead stroke may be caused by not starting in the sideways hitting stance, using little or no weight shift, providing less than full arm extension, not rotating the upper body enough, executing little or no forearm rotation, or not performing a complete follow-through.

Around-the-Head Shot

More power and deception are possible with the around-the-head shot (figure 8.2), resulting in more depth and speed on the return. The vigorous scissoring action of the legs often produces a landing force of three to four times a player's body weight on the nonracket leg. This action also initiates the player's return to midcourt.

Figure 8.2 **Around-the-Head Shot**

CONTACT

1. Contact shuttle over your nondominant shoulder

2. Let racket follow the path of the shuttle with vigorous upper-body rotation

3. Generate the majority of the force needed with forearm rotation, or pronation

4. Shift your body weight from dominant foot to nondominant foot and back again

5. Allow your hand and your wrist to slow down your racket and your arm

6. Let palm of dominant hand finish outward away from your body

Misstep

Your around-the-head shot lacks power.

Correction

Loss of power may be due to not contacting the shuttle around the head, using little or no weight shift, performing less than complete forearm rotation, not having enough shoulder flexibility, or executing a less than complete follow-through.

Misstep

You are slow to recover after hitting the around-the-head stroke.

Correction

As the shot is made and your nondominant foot hits the floor, push off toward midcourt.

The around-the-head shot requires a player to hit the shuttle over his or her nondominant shoulder. When an opponent's return is hit to the backhand side, the around-the-head shot provides a potentially strong, quick return. The body should bend slightly toward the backhand side with your weight shifted primarily to the nondominant foot. Otherwise, the stroke is executed similar to hitting the normal forehand stroke. The dominant arm swings the racket around from behind the head and almost brushes the head as the arm is extended and swung forward to meet the oncoming shuttle. Executing this shot correctly requires a high degree of shoulder flexibility. Contact the shuttle over the nondominant shoulder at the highest point possible. At contact, the body weight shifts from the nondominant foot to the dominant foot on the follow-through. The around-the-head clear, drop shot, or smash may be used as a return to intercept and quickly return a low clear hit toward the backhand side.

Often, especially in doubles play, the around-the-head stroke is executed when facing the net and requires no scissors kick to execute. These types of around-the-head shots are necessary when the shuttle is hit quickly and in a flat trajectory toward you and you have no time to change your hitting stance. The shuttle may be driven or smashed from this squared-up position and directed in a downward or horizontal path over the net.

Misstep

You lack shoulder flexibility, which prevents the racket from traveling through the complete range of motion necessary to execute the shot correctly.

Correction

Work on your flexibility. Incorporate stretching exercises into your daily routine.

Attacking Clear

During an attacking clear (figure 8.3), the racket face meets the shuttle at an angle that directs it more forward than upward. The attacking clear is a fast, quick clear that the player hits with a flat racket, slightly sooner and more out in front of the dominant shoulder. Instead of the hand leading the racket as in the normal clear, the racket and hand go out to meet the shuttle at approximately the same time. This causes the shuttle to take a flatter trajectory but one that is high enough so that the opponent cannot intercept it. He or she must move quickly to the back of the court.

Figure 8.3   Attacking Clear

CONTACT

1. Hit the shuttle out in front of your dominant shoulder
2. Angle your racket face to create a flat trajectory
3. Throw out racket and hand to meet the shuttle at the same time and direct the shuttle forward rather than upward

To hit the attacking clear, begin in a sideways hitting stance. Throw the racket up to meet the oncoming shuttle in front of your dominant shoulder. The racket face goes out to meet the shuttle and hits it in a flat trajectory. The racket follows the shuttle's path with vigorous upper-body rotation. Shift your weight from back to front, transferring your body weight from your dominant foot to your nondominant foot. The forearm rotation or pronation generates the majority of force needed. Use your hand and wrist to slow the racket and arm. Finish with the palm of your dominant hand outward away from your body.

If your attacking clear lacks power, it may be due to one of these factors:

- Not starting in the sideways hitting stance
- Little or no weight shift

- Less than full arm extension
- Not enough upper-body rotation
- Dominant hand leading the racket causing a higher than desirable return
- Little or no forearm rotation
- Less than complete follow-through

Jump Smash and Jump Drop Shot

The point of contact for the jump smash (figure 8.4) should be in front of the dominant shoulder with the racket significantly in front of the hand. The racket face leads the dominant hand and creates a downward angle into your opponent's court. A vigorous upper-body turn and simultaneous scissors kick with the legs provide additional power. The nondominant arm aids in speeding up the upper-body rotation. Forearm

Figure 8.4 **Jump Smash**

CONTACT

1. Jump into the air with the scissors kick
2. Apply vigorous upper-body rotation
3. Make contact in front of your dominant shoulder
4. Apply arm extension followed by vigorous forearm pronation
5. Have your racket face lead your hand, angling shuttle downward

pronation continues to provide the majority of the power needed. You can improve the angle for smashing by jumping in the air to hit the shuttle as soon as possible. This higher platform for initiating the smash creates a greater angle of attack and the shuttle gets to the floor faster.

Begin in a sideways hitting stance. Propel yourself into the air by flexing your legs and then immediately extending them vigorously. Throw the racket up to meet the oncoming shuttle in front of the dominant shoulder. Bring the racket face out to meet the shuttle and hit it in a flat trajectory. Follow the shuttle's path with vigorous upper-body rotation. An explosive takeoff helps to transfer momentum to the upper body,

causing vigorous upper-body rotation and scissoring leg action. The scissoring leg action adds to the transfer of momentum as the dominant leg drives forward and the nondominant leg is propelled backward. The forearm rotation or pronation generates the majority of force needed. Slow the racket and arm with the hand and wrist. Finish with the palm of the dominant hand outward away from the body.

A loss of power in the jump smash may be due to any of the following:

- Not starting in the sideways hitting stance
- Little or no weight shift

- Less than full arm extension
- Not enough upper-body rotation
- Dominant hand leading the racket causing a higher than desirable return
- Little or no forearm rotation
- Less than complete follow-through

The jump drop shot (figure 8.5) is executed exactly like the jump smash, except instead of a vigorous forearm rotation and wrist action, the action is slowed down prior to contact and the shuttle is blocked into the front court. The intention is to suggest that a smash is about to be hit.

Figure 8.5   Jump Drop Shot

CONTACT

1. Jump into the air with the scissors kick
2. Apply vigorous upper-body rotation
3. Make contact in front of your dominant shoulder but slow down swing prior to contact
4. Follow your arm extension by slower forearm pronation to block the shuttle into the frontcourt
5. Allow your racket face to lead your hand, angling shuttle downward
6. Follow through down and in line with the return

Half Smash and Fast Drop

A half smash (figure 8.6) falls somewhere between a full smash and a fast drop shot. It carries deeper in the opponent's court than the fast drop shot but not as deep as a full smash. Its reduced speed causes the shuttle to get to the floor at a steeper angle. The fast drop gets over the net faster than a normal drop shot and thus gives the opponent less time. It is particularly effective in doubles play. Instead of hitting the shuttle with a flat face, create a slice with a fast swing. This produces some deception and the return falls shorter in length.

Figure 8.6	**Half Smash**

CONTACT

1. Stand in sideways hitting stance

2. Throw your racket up to meet the oncoming shuttle in front of your dominant shoulder

3. Hit the shuttle in a downward trajectory with a slicing action, which reduces the overall speed to create the half smash effect

4. Allow the racket to follow the path of the shuttle with vigorous upper-body rotation

5. Shift your weight from back to front transferring your body weight from your dominant foot to your nondominant foot

6. Generate the majority of the force needed through forearm rotation, or pronation

7. Allow your hand and wrist to slow down your racket and arm

8. Let the palm of your dominant hand finish outward away from your body

The half smash is executed exactly like the full smash except the racket face is turned slightly to cause a slicing action, which slows down the smash considerably. The half smash gets to the floor at a slightly steeper angle and its slightly reduced speed causes the shuttle to travel less deep into the opponent's court. The target in singles is midcourt toward either sideline. In doubles, it can also be directed toward the middle and between the opponents to cause some indecision as to which partner should make the return. It can be hit from anywhere near your backcourt or near midcourt. It is hit with the intention of disguising its reduced speed and to make the opponent think that a full smash is coming. Also, in singles play its deception can result in an outright winner. In doubles, the primary intention is to get your opponents to lift the return and perhaps give you an even better opportunity to put the bird away and end the rally.

A loss of power or deception during the half smash may be due to any of the following:

- Not starting in the sideways hitting stance

- Little or no weight shift

- Less than full arm extension telegraphing your return

- Not enough upper-body rotation; square stance telegraphing your return

- Dominant hand leading the racket causing the shuttle to travel too deep into the opponent's court

- Little or no forearm rotation

- Less than complete follow-through

The fast drop should look just like the smash, except instead of fully hitting the shuttle, the fast drop is blocked and falls near or shortly past the short service line. You slow the forward swing slightly to block the shuttle down into the opponent's court. The fast drop gets over the net sooner than the normal singles drop shot. Its added speed gives your opponent less time to react and reduces the options for his or her possible returns. The path of the fast drop is definitely at a downward angle and should not have an arc or loop to its path. This fast drop gives your opponent a different look, almost a change-up effect.

Backhand Smash

The backhand smash requires proper timing, a high level of skill, and solid eye-hand coordination. When you hit a backhand smash, your goal should be to suggest an overhead clear or drop shot is about to be hit. Racket speed is the primary difference. Use the powerful stroking action of the backhand smash to put away any short returns or force your opponent to hit

returns up. A backhand smash in doubles play may also create some indecision as to which player should make the return.

As you move to the oncoming shuttle, lift the racket arm from the shoulder with the elbow up. Point the racket downward and cock your wrist. Use the backhand grip with the thumb up for added leverage. Vigorously extend the racket arm up, leading with the elbow, and rapidly rotate the forearm (supination). This forearm rotation provides most of the power. The wrist uncocks naturally and the arm fully extends (figure 8.7). The hand and racket head follow through downward and in line with the return. The racket must be moving rapidly and contact the shuttle as high as possible. The racket face must be at a downward angle.

See step 6 for more information on the backhand smash.

Figure 8.7 **Backhand Smash**

CONTACT

1. Apply backhand grip, thumb up
2. Rotate your forearm for power
3. Uncock your wrist and allow your hand and racket to follow through naturally
4. Extend your arm fully

Sliced Crosscourt Drop Shot

The fast, sliced drop differs from the basic straight-ahead drop shot in that as it reaches the net, it travels deeper into the opponent's court. It is a quicker shot, similar to a well-angled smash. This crosscourt drop shot is hit downward with the same preparatory movement as used in the smash (see figure 6.1, page 79, for the forehand smash, or figure 6.2, page 82, for the backhand smash). However, you must hit across the shuttle from left to right (figure 8.8), much like the slice serve in tennis. The racket face is angled slightly inward, approximately 40 to 45 degrees. Contact is made at about one o'clock, over your dominant shoulder with the racket slightly tilted to slide across the tip of the shuttle, creating the slicing effect. The sliced crosscourt drop shot can be hit from either the forehand or the backhand side.

Figure 8.8	Forehand Sliced Crosscourt Drop Shot

CONTACT

1. Angle racket face inward
2. Make contact over your dominant shoulder
3. Hit shuttle from left to right to create slice

Reverse Sliced Crosscourt Drop Shot

You can hit the reverse crosscourt drop shot downward with the same preparatory movement as used in the smash (see figure 6.1, page 79, for the forehand smash, or figure 6.2, page 82, for the backhand smash). However, it resembles the around-the-head shot, especially regarding the body action and landing following the shot. Throw the racket upward and strike the shuttle from right to left, creating a reverse slice effect and extreme forearm pronation (figure 8.9). The racket face is angled slightly outward, approximately 40 to 45 degrees. Contact is made at about one o'clock, over your dominant shoulder with the racket slightly tilted to slide across the tip of the shuttle, creating the slicing effect.

Figure 8.9   Reverse Sliced Crosscourt Drop Shot

CONTACT

1. Throw racket up
2. Angle racket face out slightly
3. Make contact at about one o'clock
4. Make contact over your dominant shoulder
5. Strike shuttle right to left to create slice

Backhand Crosscourt Drop Shot

Similar to the backhand smash (see figure 6.2, page 82), the sliced backhand crosscourt drop shot (figure 8.10) is hit with a vigorous backhand overhead motion that slices across the oncoming shuttle. Contact is made at about 11 o'clock and the amount of tilt or angle on the racket face determines how much angle is produced or how far sideways the shuttle will travel.

Figure 8.10   Backhand Crosscourt Drop Shot

CONTACT

1. Make contact at about 11 o'clock
2. Hit shuttle with backhand motion
3. Racket face is angled 40 to 45 degrees
4. Racket slices shuttle from left to right

The fast, sliced backhand crosscourt drop shot differs from the basic straight-ahead drop shot in that as it reaches the net, it travels deeper into the opponent's court. It is a quicker shot, similar to a well-angled backhand smash. This backhand crosscourt drop shot is hit downward with the same preparatory movement as used in the backhand smash (see figure 6.2, page 82, for the backhand smash). However, you must hit across the shuttle from right to left. The racket face is angled slightly inward, approximately 40 to 45 degrees. Contact is made at about eleven o'clock, over your dominant shoulder with the racket slightly tilted to slide across the tip of the shuttle, creating the slicing effect. The sliced backhand crosscourt drop shot should be deceptive and difficult to anticipate.

Overhead Strokes Drill 1. *Smash and Block Shot Return in Mixed Doubles*

The partner starting the rally begins with only one shuttle. This is a continuous drill. Serving from the left court, player B, a man, serves short to player A, a woman. Player A lifts the serve crosscourt and then falls back diagonally, crosscourt from the high, clear return. Player B smashes crosscourt at player A. She will attempt to block the smash return straight ahead to player B's forehand side. Player B hits the blocked down-the-line shot with a soft push shot return to midcourt. Player A then lifts a high clear to player B's right backcourt. Player B smashes crosscourt toward player A, who has retreated diagonally across from her opponent's forehand smash. She will now attempt to block the smash straight ahead to player B's backhand side. Again player B pushes or drives a soft, friendly, midcourt return. Player A returns the push with a high clear to player B's backhand or left side. The sequence continues for as long as the rally lasts. This is a continuous drill in which the male partner should attempt to execute crosscourt smashes followed by the female blocking the return straight ahead, keeping the rally going indefinitely. Returns should be flat and near enough to the partner to allow the rally to continue. Good returns should be sent either down the sideline or crosscourt near midcourt. Each rally should go for as long as possible.

To Increase Difficulty

- Player B executes push shots to both corners or drops to the net, using straight drives or crosscourt push shots. By expanding the area of play to include various corners, the players gain endurance and control for long rallies in actual games.

- The male partner may increase the pace of the smash or decrease the time allowed for his female partner to recover.

To Decrease Difficulty

- Player B executes slower push shots to both corners or slower drops to the net, using higher or softer push shots. By reducing the area of play to exclude the various corners, the player gains time and control for learning to extend the length of rallies in actual games.

- The male partner may decrease the pace of the smash or increase the time allowed for his female partner to recover.

Success Check

- Elbow leads the arm extension followed by forearm rotation on the smashes.

- Swing under control, pushing or directing the shuttle to midcourt.

- Female partner is able to control flat crosscourt and down-the-sideline blocked returns.

Score Your Success

Rally for at least 60 seconds without a miss = 10 points

Rally for 45 to 59 seconds without a miss = 5 points

Rally for 30 to 44 seconds without a miss = 1 point

Your score ____

Overhead Strokes Drill 2. *12-Shot Rallies*

These longer rallies emphasize advanced stroke production, that is, your choice of return from various locations on the court during competition. Use the following 12-shot rallies to practice your strokes and make the rally last. You may perform the drills beginning with a singles serve from the right or left side of the court. Where you begin necessarily places more emphasis on the forehand or backhand returns.

Rally 1

1. High singles serve from right court
2. Straight clear
3. Straight return clear
4. Crosscourt drop shot
5. Redrop
6. Straight clear
7. Straight clear
8. Straight clear
9. Crosscourt drop shot
10. Redrop
11. Straight clear
12. Straight clear

Rally 2

1. High singles serve from left court
2. Straight clear
3. Straight return clear
4. Crosscourt drop shot
5. Redrop
6. Straight clear
7. Straight clear
8. Straight clear
9. Crosscourt drop shot
10. Redrop
11. Straight clear
12. Straight clear

Rally 3

1. High singles serve from right court
2. Straight clear
3. Straight return clear
4. Crosscourt smash
5. Redrop
6. Straight clear
7. Straight clear
8. Straight clear
9. Crosscourt smash
10. Redrop
11. Straight clear
12. Straight clear

Rally 4

1. High singles serve from left court
2. Straight clear
3. Straight return clear
4. Crosscourt smash
5. Redrop
6. Straight clear
7. Straight clear
8. Straight clear
9. Crosscourt smash
10. Redrop
11. Straight clear
12. Straight clear

Success Check

- Hit clears high and deep.
- Hit smashes downward with some pace.
- Let drop shots fall close to the top of the net.
- Hit drive shots quickly and in a flat trajectory.

Score Your Success

Complete three or four rallies without missing = 10 points

Complete two rallies without missing = 5 points

Complete one rally without missing = 1 point

Your score ___

NET PLAY

Net play adds a new dimension to your badminton game. The net provides a barrier to separate you from your opponent. It also provides a target for net play. Because your returns must clear the net and the net is five feet high, shots at the net necessarily give your opponent more time. You must hit returns before they touch the floor, so time is of the essence. More advanced shots at the net should make your opponent move and increase the likelihood he or she will commit an error.

Both singles and doubles play require some play at the net. The drop shot at the net is used more often in singles than in doubles. However, because you have a partner in doubles, you can play more aggressively toward the net. Slow drop shots initiated either at the net or from the backcourt give your doubles opponents more time to react and therefore are less attractive in doubles than they would be in singles. Singles is more of a running game and requires more patience. The slower drop shots require the singles player to run more and cover more court.

Tumble Drop Shot

The tumble drop shot (figure 8.11) can be hit with either a forehand or a backhand motion. Brushing underneath the bird in a sideways motion will make the shuttle spin or tumble as it goes over the net, making it much more difficult to hit cleanly. This tumbling action forces the player making the return to let gravity straighten out the shuttle's flight. Time is needed to allow the shuttle to right itself and fall back to a vertical path. The opponent must allow the shuttle to fall closer to the floor in order to contact the tip of the shuttle with his or her racket for a possible return. The tumble drop shot looks very much like the drop shots covered in step 5 except the bird tumbles as it crosses the net.

Figure 8.11 Tumble Drop Shot

CONTACT

1. Pivot and reach with your dominant foot and hand in the direction of the shuttle

2. Place your racket under the dropping shuttle

3. Put your wrist in laid back, or cocked, position

4. Contact the shuttle as high as possible and brush it in a sideways, underhand motion to make it tumble or spin

5. Place your weight forward on your dominant foot

Underhand Crosscourt Drop Shot

It's common to lift or bump over drop shots at the net as close to the top of the net as possible. However, often the shuttle is reached at a much lower point and this provides an opportunity for an underhanded crosscourt drop shot return (figure 8.12). The crosscourt drop shot may be hit with either a forehand or a backhand motion. This lower contact point requires one to angle the racket face approximately 45 degrees in order to send the shuttle in a sideways path. The shuttle should then travel diagonally across your side of the net, peaking at the top of the net and then falling on your opponent's side inside the court. This type of return requires your opponent to move quickly in order to get the return, but the shuttle also stays in the air longer so your opponent will have more time to get there.

Figure 8.12   Underhand Crosscourt Drop Shot

CONTACT

1. Pivot and reach with your dominant foot and hand in the direction of the shuttle
2. Place your racket under the dropping shuttle
3. Put your wrist in laid back, or cocked, position
4. Contact the shuttle as high as possible and angle the shuttle in a sideways, underhand motion to direct the shuttle crosscourt
5. Your weight should be forward on your dominant foot

Drop Shot Drill 1. *Forehand Corner*

A coach or feeder stands at the far right or far left, short service line on the opposite side of the net. He or she lifts the shuttle to the forehand corner. The player executes a drop shot only to the corner in which the coach is standing. The player should hit 10 forehand drop shots and 10 backhand drop shots.

To Increase Difficulty

- Player must execute drop shots to both corners or the net, using straight drops and crosscourt drop shots. By expanding the area of play to include various corners, the player gains endurance and control for long rallies in actual games.

Success Check

- Execute the underhand drop shot motion.
- Place your racket under the oncoming drop shot, and lift from your shoulder.
- Reach with your dominant hand and foot.
- Finish palm up on your forehand and palm down on your backhand.

Score Your Success

Complete 10 forehand drop shots in a row = 5 points

Complete 10 backhand drop shots in a row = 5 points

Your score ___

Drop Shot Drill 2. *Alternate Corners*

A coach or feeder stands at the far right or far left, short service line on the opposite side of the net. He or she lifts the shuttle to the forehand or backhand corner, alternating from one to the other. The player executes a drop shot to the corner of the net where the coach is standing, using straight drops and crosscourt drop shots.

Success Check

- Execute the underhand drop shot motion.
- Place your racket under the oncoming drop shot and lift from your shoulder.
- Reach with your dominant hand and foot.
- Finish palm up on your forehand and palm down on your backhand.

Score Your Success

Complete 10 forehand drop shots in a row = 5 points

Complete 10 backhand drop shots in a row = 5 points

Your score ___

Drop Shot Drill 3. *Three Corners*

A coach or feeder stands at the far right or far left, short service line on the opposite side of the net. The coach or feeder may direct the shuttle to any of three corners. The player hits a drop shot to the corner of the net where the coach is standing.

Success Check

- Execute the underhand drop shot motion.
- Place your racket under the oncoming drop shot and lift from your shoulder.
- Reach with your dominant hand and foot.
- Finish palm up on your forehand and palm down on your backhand.

Score Your Success

Complete 10 forehand drop shots in a row = 5 points

Complete 10 backhand drop shots in a row = 5 points

Your score ___

SERVE AND RETURN OF SERVE

The serve and the return of serve are the most important single strokes in badminton because every point is initiated with the serve and return of serve. The new rally point scoring system ensures a point is made on every rally played.

The advanced serves and service returns covered in this step require more skill and racket control. They are also more aggressive and are designed to place additional pressure on the opponent. These advanced serves and service returns will give your opponent a different look and feature an element of surprise. These serves and returns should be extremely consistent and accurate with little chance for error. Some serves and returns of serve incorporate deception in their delivery as well to keep the opponent off balance. This deception prevents the opponent from attacking on the serve or return and helps to reduce the probability of you making errors. Instead, it should increase the probability of your opponent making mistakes or errors during his or her serves and returns of serve.

Reverse Brushed Serve

The reverse brushed serve incorporates some of the characteristics of an old, now illegal serve of the 1970s in which the feathers were contacted first on the serve. Now on a legal serve you must contact the shuttle tip first. But an option is to hold the shuttle with your nonracket hand, grasping it with two or three fingers inside the feathered skirt with your thumb outside and the tip pointed back toward your body (figure 8.13a). Although the reverse brushed serve is commonly delivered from the backhand service position, it can also be done with a forehand delivery. As the racket comes forward to contact the shuttle, the racket is beveled slightly (figure 8.13b), putting a subtle underspin on the shuttle, causing it to waffle or gyrate and giving the receiver a different look as the shuttle leaves the server's racket and travels over the net. This flip-like effect is designed to reduce the receiver's ability to play an aggressive return of the serve.

The follow-through (figure 8.13c) is down and across the tip of the shuttle from left to right for a right-handed player. The racket finishes down and to the right with the wrist and hand finishing palm downward as a result of the beveling action of the racket face at contact. The racket head continues in an arc and is brought up with the racket in front of the body to get ready for any possible return by the opponent.

| **Figure 8.13** | **Reverse Brushed Serve** |

PREPARATION

1. Hold shuttle in your nonracket hand
2. Place two or three fingers inside the shuttle's feathered skirt
3. Place your thumb outside the feathers
4. Point the shuttle's tip toward your body

a

b

c

EXECUTION

1. Swing your racket forward to meet the tip of the shuttle
2. Brush shuttle with slicing action by using a downward swing with a slight beveling of the racket face
3. Hit the shuttle with underspin
4. Allow the shuttle to flip or waffle slightly as it leaves the racket face

FOLLOW-THROUGH

1. Your racket head travels down and across the tip of the shuttle from left to right for a right-handed player
2. Your racket finishes down and to the right
3. Your wrist and hand finish palm down as a result of the beveling action of the racket face at contact
4. Your racket head continues in an arc
5. Your racket finishes in front of your body, ready for your opponent's return

Misstep

You make contact above the waist or with the racket head above the racket hand, resulting in an illegal serve.

Correction

Make sure you contact the shuttle below the waist and keep the racket head below any part of the racket hand.

Half-Court Push Return

The half-court push return (figure 8.14) is played at or above the net and directs the bird down into an open spot in your opponent's half-court. The shuttle is pushed, not hit. It is a very effective return in doubles play. It may be used occasionally in singles play but it is essential for doubles play.

The shuttle is placed past the net player, forcing the backcourt player to reach for the shuttle below net height and hit the shuttle up.

The half-court push return should also cause some indecision as to which partner should make the return. The sooner and higher the shuttle is contacted, the more sharply and steeply all net returns can be made.

Figure 8.14 | Half-Court Push Return

EXECUTION

1. Push the shuttle, don't hit it
2. Direct the shuttle toward the sideline near midcourt
3. Maintain up-and-back offensive position

Misstep

You overhit the return or swing too hard, sending the return out of bounds.

Correction

Be aware of the boundaries for your game (singles or doubles). Learn to hit the shuttle with enough force to place it where you want it to go but also with enough finesse to keep it in bounds.

Serve and Service Return Drill 1. *Half-Court Push Return*

Player A begins by serving a short serve across the net. Player A's partner stands in ready position behind player A. The receiver hits a push into the midcourt of the doubles alley beyond the server's reach, requiring the server's partner to get the return.

After the receiver completes 10 forehand pushes and 10 backhand pushes, rotate positions and roles. Be sure to perform the drill from both service courts. Each receiver should complete 10 forehand pushes and 10 backhand pushes.

Success Check

- Push the shuttle, don't hit it.
- Direct the shuttle toward the sideline near midcourt.
- Maintain up-and-back offensive position.

Hit at least 10 or more forehand returns without a miss = 5 points

Hit at least 10 backhand returns without a miss = 5 points

Your score ___

Serve and Service Return Drill 2. *Push Shot Rally*

The partner starting the rally needs to begin with only one or two shuttles. Player A will hit only down-the-line push shot returns, and player B will hit only soft drive shot returns to midcourt. Player A begins by pushing or driving a flat, friendly midcourt drive down the sideline to player B's forehand. Player B returns the drive with a soft midcourt drive to player A's backhand side. Player A then pushes his or her return down the sideline to player B's forehand. Player B hits a forehand push shot return to player A at midcourt. Player B must recover quickly to centercourt. This is a continuous drill in which both partners should attempt to execute as many soft drive or push shot returns as possible, keeping the rally going indefinitely. Returns should be flat and near enough to the partner to allow the rally to continue. Good returns should be sent either down the sideline or crosscourt near midcourt. Each rally should go for as long as possible. When the rally ends, change the sequence to allow player B to hit backhand push shots and player A to hit forehand returns down the sideline.

Success Check

- The elbow leads the arm extension, followed by forearm rotation.
- Swing under control, pushing or directing the shuttle to midcourt.
- Hit flat crosscourt and down-the-sideline exchanges.

Score Your Success

Rally for at least 20 returns without a miss = 10 points

Rally for 15 to 19 returns without a miss = 5 points

Rally for 10 to 14 returns without a miss = 1 point

Your score ___

DECEPTION

The ability to camouflage your shots is a very important skill. All overhead strokes should look the same up until contact with the shuttle is made. This disguises which shot is coming. This deception is designed to win the rally outright or to force a weak return. The basic strokes must be executed with the same preparatory movements. The most important aspect of concealing a shot is in the upper-body or shoulder rotation. Deception requires a similar starting position with the feet and should include a vigorous upper-body turn on all overhead strokes, especially the overhead drop shot. With the same preparation and hitting movement, it will be difficult for your opponent to anticipate your overhead returns.

Underhand returns can also be deceptive. You could hold the return of a drop shot from the underhand position and then change the return. By getting to the shuttle early, placing the racket under the oncoming shuttle, and holding it there, you can then watch your opponent in your peripheral vision to see if he or she waits until you hit or if he or she anticipates your shot. If your opponent remains stationary and waits, simply drop the shuttle over the net. If he or she moves, then change from the drop shot return to a pitch-out or underhand clear.

Misstep

Overuse of deception can lead to excessive errors in its execution. Overuse can also be less effective.

Correction

Deception is most effective due to the element of surprise. You can go to the well too often and become predictable. Strategically use deception, but don't overdo it.

Hold Return During Overhead Motion

As you move to the oncoming shuttle, raise your racket arm and cock your wrist. On the forehand, place your racket behind the shoulders between the shoulder blades.

You can initiate the normal overhead motion with the rapid upward extension of your racket arm. By slightly delaying your forearm rotation and subsequent wrist action you have the ability to hold your overhead stroke. The racket arm moves forward, but the racket is left back and cocked.

This holding action causes a brief moment of indecision in the opponent. He or she may be unable to recognize which stroke is being made. If the opponent moves either direction or is caught leaning one way or another, the shot may be changed or directed to another part of the court. Often, the opponent has to take extra steps and he or she has the sensation of being "jerked" around the court.

Hold Return of Drop Shot

You can create another form of deception by getting to the shuttle early, placing the racket under the oncoming shuttle's path, and holding it there. Then watch your opponent in your peripheral vision to see if he or she waits until you hit or if he or she anticipates your shot. If

he or she remains stationary and waits, simply drop the shuttle over the net. If your opponent moves, then change from the drop shot return and hit the shuttle to the backcourt. Simply drop the racket quickly and pitch the shuttle to the backcourt. This generally prevents your opponent from gaining any advantage by trying to anticipate which return you will make.

Hold Return of Short Serve

Another form of deception can be created by getting to the shuttle early on the service return, placing the racket under the oncoming shuttle, and holding it there. Watch your opponent in your peripheral vision to see if he or she waits until you hit or if he or she anticipates your shot. Move your racket forward as if to hit a normal drop shot or push shot return of serve. Wave the racket face at the shuttle, intentionally missing it, then drop the racket quickly and pitch the shuttle crosscourt.

Misdirect the Shot

The term *misdirection* is somewhat self-explanatory. This is the ability to look or give a bodily movement that fakes the opponent into believing you are hitting the shuttle one way when you are instead hitting it to another place. You can accomplish this feinting action with your eyes, your racket hand, or torso movements. A waving action with your racket prior to hitting the shuttle allows you to feint one way and hit another way. That is why it is not allowed during the serve. It would give the server an unfair advantage.

Misdirection is accomplished primarily by upper-body rotation on all overhead strokes. Misdirection on returns of serve or drop shots at the net are most often accomplished by subtle changes in the angle of the racket face. Dipping or slipping the racket face in and then out from under the oncoming shuttle may cause the opponent to take unnecessary steps or to get faked out.

Extremely hard hit returns in doubles provide numerous opportunities to misdirect your shot. Slight changes in the angle of the racket face allow for what seems to be miraculous saves. Elite doubles players have often learned these skills so well that they do not have to think about them. This is called a *conditioned reflex*. Often in sports, we use the term *react*, and often athletes do react surprisingly well to all forms of stimulus. But most of the time, elite athletes have been in that situation before and have practiced potential returns in that situation thousands of times. They instinctively hit the correct shot or the shot that is seemingly the best return. This is a learned skill.

Overuse of deception can be less effective. Deception is most effective due to its element of surprise. Elite players often get accustomed to playing against deception or players with a certain style of play and can develop a habituated response. Instinctive play can be both positive and negative. If you become too predictable, the elite player will recognize this pattern and take advantage of it. However, most world-class players can hit an array of shots from any one area. They are usually very unpredictable, which does not allow their opponents to anticipate potential returns.

Push Into the Body

The half-court push return of serve is normally placed out to either side of the server. The push into the body return of serve (figure 8.15) is a change from the typical side court placement that is employed in doubles. In doubles, the server normally serves short and plays aggressively toward the net. If you push the return straight at the server, the server will have little time to react. Often you can "handcuff" him. The push into the body can be executed from either the forehand or backhand side, but the shuttle must be contacted as soon as possible just as it comes over the net. The push into the body return also limits your opponent's possible angle of return. You must be ready for the return because it will probably cross near the center of the net. This return is almost never used in singles play.

Figure 8.15 Push Into the Body

CONTACT

1. Make contact as soon as the shuttle crosses the net
2. Direct return toward your opponent's nondominant shoulder

Misstep

You overhit the return or swing too hard, sending the return out of bounds.

Correction

Be aware of the boundaries for your game. Hit the shuttle with enough force to place it where you want it to go but also with enough finesse to keep it in bounds. The push into the body return of serve is meant to be a controlled return, subtle—not a smash. An error here gives your opponent a point.

Deception Drill 1. *Hold Return of Short Serve*

A server sends a friendly short serve across the net. Move to the shuttle and put your racket underneath the shuttle as it crosses the net. After serving, the server should move to a different area of the court. Using your peripheral vision, watch the server's motion and hold your return until the server stops moving. Hit the return away from the server. Complete 10 hold returns.

Success Check

- Get to the shuttle early.
- Place your racket underneath the shuttle, in its path.
- Watch the server, using your peripheral vision.
- Send the return away from the server.

Successfully return 10 or more serves away from server = 10 points

Successfully return 6 to 9 serves away from server = 5 points

Successfully return 1 to 5 serves away from server = 1 point

Your score ___

Deception Drill 2. *Short Serve and Push Into the Body Return*

A server sends a short serve across the net while his or her partner stands in ready position. The receiver hits a push into the body return, sending the shuttle back toward the server before the server has time to recover and get in position. After the receiver completes 10 forehand pushes and 10 backhand pushes, rotate positions and roles. Be sure to perform the drill from both service courts. Each receiver should complete 10 forehand pushes and 10 backhand pushes.

Success Check

- Make contact with the shuttle as soon as it crosses the net.
- Send the return right back to the server.

Score Your Success

Complete 10 forehand pushes into the body = 5 points

Complete 10 backhand pushes into the body = 5 points

Your score ___

TRICK SHOTS

You can learn and practice many fun trick shots that can be hit when facing the net or with your back to the net. Trick shots—such as the around-the-back and the between-the-legs smash returns—and shots designed to let the shuttle drop below the normal hitting position can surprise an unsuspecting opponent.

Around-the-Back Smash Return

This trick shot is done when you are facing the net. This return requires the opponent's smash to be directed downward and toward your backhand side. With an underhand hit, contact is made with the shuttle as it passes by your body (figure 8.16) on the nondominant side and the shuttle is blocked or driven back over the net.

Figure 8.16 Around-the-back return of a smash.

125

Between-the-Legs Smash Return

This return is performed while facing the net. This return requires the opponent's smash to be directed downward and directly at you. With an underhand hit, contact is made with the shuttle as it passes between your legs (figure 8.17) and the shuttle is blocked back over the net.

Figure 8.17 Between-the-legs return of a smash.

Between-the-Legs Clear Return

This return is hit when your back is to the net. This shot must travel past you. You must allow the shuttle to fall to knee level or below. With an underhand hit, make contact with the shuttle with your body between the shuttle and the net (figure 8.18). The return is directed between your legs with your back to the net. A drop shot or clear may be returned with this shot.

Figure 8.18 Between-the-legs return of a clear.

Misstep

You make contact above the waist or with the racket head above the racket hand, resulting in your body interfering with the return.

Correction

Make sure you contact the shuttle below the waist and make contact with the shuttle between the knees.

Below-the-Waist Underhand Clear Return

This shot must travel past you. You must allow the shuttle to fall to waist level or below. With an underhand, forehand hit on your backhand side, make contact with the shuttle with your body between the shuttle and the net (figure 8.19). Complete the return with inverse rotation of the dominant arm on a forehand hit below the waist and with your back to the net. A drop shot or clear may be returned with this shot.

Figure 8.19 Underhand return of a clear to the backhand, hit below the waist with inverse rotation.

Trick Shot Drill 1. *Around-the-Back Smash Return*

Perform 10 around-the-back smash returns. Have a partner hit a friendly smash to you. The smash needs to be directed downward toward your backhand side. Return the smash with an around-the-back return. Perform returns from both service courts.

Success Check

- Make contact with the shuttle as it passes your body on the nondominant side.
- Block or drive the shuttle back over the net.

Score Your Success

Complete 10 around-the-back smash returns = 5 points

Your score ___

Trick Shot Drill 2. *Between-the-Legs Return*

Perform 10 forehand returns between the legs while facing the net and 10 forehand returns between the legs with your back to the net. Have a partner hit a smash downward and aimed directly at you. Direct the return between your legs back over the net. Perform returns from both service courts.

Success Check

- Make contact with the shuttle between your legs.
- Be patient as you allow the shuttle to fall to knee level or lower.
- Block or drive the shuttle back over the net.

Complete 10 forehand returns between the legs while facing the net = 5 points

Complete 10 forehand returns between the legs with your back to the net = 5 points

Your score ____

Trick Shot Drill 3. *Below the Waist Underhand Clear Return*

Have a partner hit a clear to your backhand side. Allow the shot to travel past you and fall to waist level or lower. Make contact with the shuttle with your back to the net, hitting an underhand forehand to send the shuttle back over the net. Perform 10 forehand underhand clear returns. Be sure to perform the drill from both service courts.

Success Check

- Be patient as you allow the shuttle to fall to waist level or lower.
- Return the shuttle with your back to the net.
- Hit an underhand forehand shot, using an inverse rotation of your dominant arm.

Score Your Success

Complete 10 forehand underhand returns = 10 points

Complete 5 to 9 forehand underhand returns = 5 points

Complete 1 to 4 forehand underhand returns = 1 point

Your score ____

SUCCESS SUMMARY OF ADVANCED TECHNIQUES

This step includes skills, techniques, and drills designed for the athlete who wishes to play at the elite level. A higher level of athletic ability and training is required. Beginning and intermediate level players need to master the basic skills and fundamentals before pursuing these more advanced skills and techniques, although they may enjoy trying them anyway for fun and practice. Competitive players will need these techniques, but recreational players may never be required to use them extensively.

Overhead Strokes Drills

1. Smash and Block Shot Return in Mixed Doubles   ___ out of 10

2. 12-Shot Rallies   ___ out of 10

Drop Shot Drills

1. Forehand Corner   ___ out of 10

2. Alternate Corners   ___ out of 10

3. Three Corners   ___ out of 10

Serve and Service Return Drills

1. Half-Court Push Return   ___ out of 10

2. Push Shot Rally   ___ out of 10

Deception Drills

1. Hold Return of Short Serve   ___ out of 10

2. Short Serve and Push Into the Body Return   ___ out of 10

Trick Shot Drills

1. Around-the-Back Smash Return   ___ out of 5

2. Between-the-Legs Return   ___ out of 10

3. Forehand Underhand Clear Return   ___ out of 10

Total   ___ *out of 115*

Beginning and intermediate players who chose to try this step just for fun can move to the next step without tallying their scores. Advanced players should score at least 90 points out of a possible 115 before moving on the next step. If you scored fewer than 90 points, redo the drills that gave you trouble. Consult with a coach, instructor, or experienced player to improve your advanced techniques.

The next step on scoring strategies introduces concepts relative to the new rally point scoring system. Tactics for both singles and doubles play will be discussed. Strategy specifically related to the rally point scoring system will be covered in detail. Because the new scoring is much faster and a point is scored on every rally, every error is magnified and there are fewer opportunities to overcome a poor start. More emphasis is placed on conservative play and reducing the number of unforced errors.

Tactics and Strategies

One of the most important aspects of badminton play is the ability to make decisions during a rally. Your ability to execute numerous shots accurately and consistently is sometimes referred to as *stroke production*. You can improve stroke production by practicing certain situations or a specific sequence of action.

Another means of improving badminton play is to observe successful players and critique their play. Note weaknesses that are common to most players or tendencies they might have from certain areas of their court. You can determine some weaknesses by scouting a potential opponent before playing against him or her or during warm-up before the match. Take advantage of any discernible weakness in your opponent's game.

To be successful in singles play, beginners must learn to sustain a rally. Most beginners have not learned to slice or cut their returns, to tumble the bird at the net, or to use much deception. Therefore, a beginner's strategy is very basic: Try to outlast your opponent. Keep the shuttle in play and wait for your opponent to make a mistake. A good way to help improve steadiness is to hit high, deep returns and to give yourself plenty of margin for error at the net. The following are other important elements of strategy to develop after gaining some degree of racket control:

- Hitting most birds deep into your opponent's court
- Hitting most returns to your opponent's weaker side, which is usually his or her backhand
- Moving your opponent around the court by hitting the bird from side to side and up and back
- Emphasizing placement and depth rather than speed on returns, which should result in fewer errors
- Changing the pace during play
- Never changing a winning strategy and always changing a losing strategy
- Making all your overhead strokes look the same because deception is a key part of becoming a better player

Tactics are deliberate efforts by you or your opponent to either win points or regain serve. For your strategy to be effective, you must play to your strengths and away from your opponent's strengths, if possible. If your opponents lack speed or endurance, attempt to make them run to tire them out. Since most players do not have as strong a backhand as they do a forehand, hit the majority of your shots to your opponent's backhand. If you are not very fit, try to attack quickly and make your rallies as short as possible by smashing or hitting outright winners. You may wish to be aggressive on your serve and safer, more conservative, on your opponent's serve. However, any error will result in a point for your opponent. Also, learn the singles or doubles boundaries well so you do not play any of your opponent's returns that would have been out.

STRATEGY UNDER THE RALLY POINT SCORING SYSTEM

In 2006, the BWF adopted the rally point scoring system for all sanctioned events. The USAB Board of Directors voted to adopt this policy for all USAB national ranking tournaments. (Non-ranking tournaments that wish to be sanctioned by USAB are not required to use rally points at this time.) In rally point scoring, all games are played to 21 points, replacing the older method of playing games to 15 and to 11 points and eliminating the unique concept of setting. The rationale for this change was to make the sport more marketable to spectators and television as well as to improve its acceptance and understanding by the general population. Preliminary observations seem to indicate match times may be reduced by as much as 25 percent. The rally scoring system requires players to be more alert and to score quickly in these abbreviated games. Athletes are required to adapt to a new strategy for winning matches. Spectators will also benefit from this exciting and potentially pressure-packed format.

Singles Strategy Under Rally Point Scoring

You win the coin toss, so what should you elect to do: serve, receive, or choose a side? If one side is better than the other, make the same choice as with the old scoring system: choose the bad side. Court conditions and the ability to see due to a light background, reflections, lighting or the presence of windows determine which side of the court is better. If you win the first game, you have the advantage of playing and likely winning the match while playing the second game on the good side. If you lose the first game, you play the second game on the good side, thus increasing your chances of winning the second game of the match. Your confidence and execution of play should be better on the good side. Also a change in strategy learned from the first game loss may enhance the opportunity to win the second game and even up the match. In the third and final game, your newer, winning strategy may allow you to play successfully even while on the bad side. When you switch sides at the 11-point mark of the third game, you will move to the good side of the net. This good side could provide increased confidence and may allow you to close out the final game and win the match.

But what if your opponent wins the toss and selects the bad side first? What should you do, serve or receive? You should elect to receive the serve. Winning a rally is much easier when a player is receiving rather than serving. First, the server has to hit the serve in the appropriate space, delivering the serve to the proper court, or the server loses the point outright. Second, the serve in badminton generally puts the server in a defensive position. Because the server hits the shuttle up and over the net, the receiver has the first chance to make an offensive shot. Thus the receiver has the better chance of controlling and winning any rally.

However, some players like to dictate or control the pace of play. A player who serves aggressively and likes to put pressure on the receiver might choose to serve first. Some beginning and intermediate players might be tempted by the idea of serving first and taking an early lead, but remember you can score by receiving also. In either case, by taking an early lead, you may gain a psychological edge on your opponent. It may simply be that you are more comfortable and confident by initiating the serve from your side.

Rally scoring places even more emphasis on the service return in singles. Because the long serve is essentially a defensive shot, it is important to hit an offensive return that will force your opponent to move but also leave you room for error. The two best methods of return are the attacking clear and the fast drop shot. A safe, conservative return that keeps your opponent honest is of extreme importance. Use one of the following options for returning the long singles serve of a right-handed opponent:

- From the right court, hit an attacking clear to your opponent's backhand side, a fast drop straight ahead, or a fast crosscourt drop shot.
- From the left court, hit an attacking clear straight ahead down your opponent's forehand side, an attacking clear crosscourt, or a fast drop shot straight ahead to your opponent's forehand side.

Misstep

Your serve or return of serve is poor or out of bounds, giving your opponent an easy score.

Correction

Keep the shuttle in play. Conservative serves and returns of serve place the pressure on your opponent. Return your opponent's serve with a purpose, but make it a safe return that makes them move and gives you time to recover to midcourt.

For a left-handed opponent, the returns would be the same but from opposite courts.

Because the rally favors the receiver, rally point scoring potentially makes matches closer than traditional scoring. The better player is forced to win most of the points while serving the shuttle. Under the traditional scoring system, although the better player had to win all of his or her points while serving, the player did not lose points if he or she lost a rally while serving. Rally point scoring seems to favor the lesser-skilled player.

Rally point scoring affects singles strategy in other ways. In general, rally point scoring makes play more conservative. Risky or poorly executed shots cause you to not only lose the rally but also lose a point. Perhaps the most risky shot in singles is hitting a return that is designed to just barely clear the net. If this shot is hit a little too short, you lose a point. However, if you hit the return with excessive height over the net, you give your opponent an easy put away shot. In general, rally scoring favors a player who consistently hits clear shots near the back boundary line. If you clear to within a foot of the back line, you have more time and your opponent will be less able to make an effective return. A player must adjust his or her target further inward when hitting returns to the extreme corners of the court. A smash directed at the sideline may go wide, causing the loss of a point, while a smash targeted to within a foot or so inside the sideline provides more margin of error for the shot maker.

Misstep

Your serve and return of serve are not consistent and produce too many errors. You have difficulty scoring points.

Correction

Vary the speed and placement of your serve and return of serve. Mix in some short, drive, or flick serves as a change of pace. Try not to let your opponent get comfortable with your serve.

Doubles Strategy Under Rally Point Scoring

In doubles if you win the toss, what should you elect to do? Serve, receive, or take a side? The strategy is the same as in singles and for the same reason. Your first choice is to take the bad side. Your second choice is to receive serve. You should never elect to serve first.

In doubles, a team must designate who will start in the odd and even courts. If your team is serving first, you maximize your team's chances of winning points by having your best server start the match from the even side. If your team is receiving the serve during the initial rally of the game, there are two schools of thought. The first thought is to put your best service receiver in the even court. This strategy gives you the best chance of winning the initial rally. Another starting strategy for the receiving team is to place their better server in the odd court. The

player on the receiving team in the odd court will be the first player to serve for the receiving team once they win a rally. By having the better server in the odd position, you maximize the scoring opportunities for the receiving team.

Rally scoring has little effect on the style of play in doubles. Successful doubles players should attempt to complement each other. Doubles teams either win together or lose together. They work in tandem, attempting to set up each other for a smash or putaway. Shots are often directed at an opponent's body or between players. This creates some indecision as to which opponent will make the return. Aggressive returns or shots directed toward the sideline may cause an error or a wide return. This results in automatic points for the opposing team. Perhaps the greatest impact that rally point scoring has had on doubles is to make matches closer, for the stronger team is forced to win the most points while having to serve defensively.

Tactics Drill 1. *Short Serve–Push Return*

Player A serves short to player B. Player B returns this short serve with a push return to his or her partner's backhand or forehand side alley (figure 9.1). This is not a rally. Player A serves until player B accomplishes five good returns toward his or her backhand or forehand side alley. This pushed

return should carry beyond his or her partner's short service line. After five good returns have been made, player B should serve short to player A and allow him or her to make five good push returns of serve.

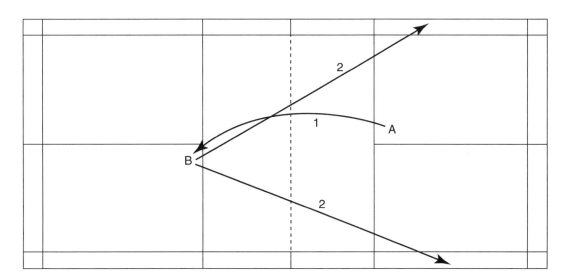

Figure 9.1 Short serve–push return.

Success Check

- Serves cross over close to top of net.
- Push returns travel to near midcourt, past short service line.

Score Your Success

Hit 30 good push returns = 10 points

Hit 20 to 29 good push returns = 5 points

Hit 10 to 19 good push returns = 1 point

Your score ___

Tactics Drill 2. *Short Serve–Net Drop Shot*

Player A serves short to player B. Player B returns this short serve with a drop shot at the net (figure 9.2) to his or her partner's backhand side alley or returns this short serve with a net drop shot return to his or her partner's forehand side alley. This is not a rally. Player A serves until player B accomplishes five good returns toward his or her backhand or forehand side alley. This pushed return should carry into his or her partner's backhand side alley to be considered a good return. After five good returns have been made, player B should serve short to player A and allow him or her to make five good net drop shot returns of serve to his or her backhand.

To Increase Difficulty

- Tumble drop shot returns instead of bumping or lifting them over.

Success Check

- Serves cross over close to top of net.
- Drop shot returns travel close to net and fall toward floor.

Score Your Success

Hit 30 good drop shot returns = 10 points

Hit 20 to 29 good drop shot returns = 5 points

Hit 10 to 19 good drop shot returns = 1 point

Your score ___

Figure 9.2 Short serve–net drop shot drill.

TACTICAL PRACTICE

The development of badminton skill requires some degree of individual dedication and proper instruction from a knowledgeable coach before a player begins to play with confidence. Badminton is different from other racket sports, such as tennis, in that the majority of power and control is generated with forearm rotation with the wrist being the action point. It is important to execute strokes with the full length of the racket shaft. The player's arm should be fully extended at contact in order to maximize the power applied to the shuttlecock. A common mistake made by beginners is to impact the shuttlecock too close to the upper body instead of at the full extension of the arm. This short-arm effect causes a loss of power and deception.

All overhead strokes should be executed with the same basic overhand throwing motion. From a sideways hitting stance, the upper body should rotate as the racket arm is extended upward to make contact with the shuttle. The nondominant arm is also raised and helps to speed up the rotation of the upper body. The fundamental basis of the badminton overhead motion may be mastered with repeated effort and exercise in the following drills. Each session can be about 5 to 10 minutes per skill. You may find it difficult in the beginning but you will develop additional control and skill over time. Stroke production is

the ability to reproduce a sequence of returns in random order with consistency and control.

Soohyun Bang was a very successful, internationally ranked badminton singles player for South Korea. She participated in two Olympic Games, receiving the silver medal in 1992 in Barcelona and the gold medal in Atlanta in 1996. She became the number-one-ranked women's singles player in the world. She suggests the following drills for developing badminton singles play. Doubles players can also benefit from this practice. The following drills are stated in reference to what the player is doing. The coach or feeder is alternating between hitting a net shot and clearing deep.

Clear

You can counter your opponent's offensive stroke with a long clear toward the back line (figure 9.3). This shot will give you time to recover and will make your opponent consume more energy by forcing him or her away from the middle of the court. Simulate game-like situations by repetitive exercise for each stroke with proper footwork.

To practice this tactic, a coach or partner is stationary in one corner near the back line. You start and end in the middle of court. Your

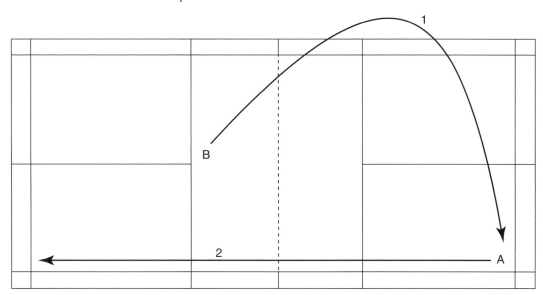

Figure 9.3 Long clear toward back line.

partner hits a long clear stroke to a corner as you move toward the corner. After you hit a clear stroke back to your partner, try to get back to the middle of the court before you hit your next stroke. Your partner should alternate which corner he or she hits to. You can hit strokes in a set pattern (for example, straight or crosscourt) or hit them randomly at your partner's discre-

tion. You are learning stroke production and the ability to sustain a rally. This practice can be made more game-like by extending the rally as long as possible. By hitting in a set pattern, you develop consistent stroke production. By practicing with random returns, you develop the ability to change on your feet or diversify your style of play.

Misstep

Your stroke production is poor; you cannot sustain a rally.

Correction

Use all four corners of your opponent's court for your returns, but give yourself plenty of room for error. When in doubt, clear!

Drop Shot

The drop shot can be used to keep your opponent on his or her toes for your every stroke, especially strokes from the back line. The drop shot is useful when your opponent uses a clear stroke to return the shuttlecock very high (figure 9.4). You have to be able to disguise the drop shot by hitting it with the same arm motion and speed as the clear stroke. If the drop shot is executed differently from the clear shot, it becomes too predictable. This may allow your opponent to anticipate your drop shot and turn it into an easy offensive opportunity. Because the drop shot is used more often during a singles

match than in doubles, it is very important to keep the overhead motion similar for both shots. The key point is to keep your swing concise and use a quick wrist action.

To practice the drop shot, your partner is stationary near the service line. You will move between the middle of the court and the back corner near the back line. You may switch sides after a while to get used to both corners. Once you are comfortable with the straight-ahead stroke, vary the direction by hitting the bird toward the opposite service line. The degree of difficulty will go up when you can hit alternating strokes, for example, straight and then diagonal. This is similar to game-like conditions.

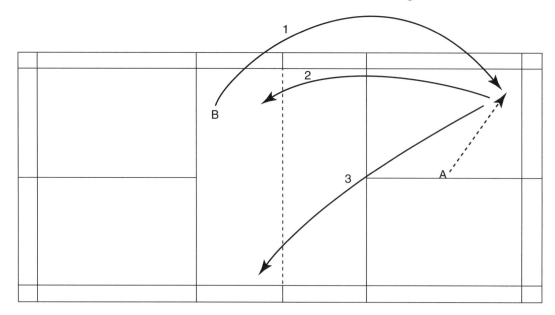

Figure 9.4 Drop shot return after a clear.

Misstep

You fail to return to centercourt and are out of position for your opponent's return.

Correction

As soon as you make your return, recover to centercourt.

Overhead Drop Shot and Hairpin at the Net

The drop shot can be used to keep your opponent off guard for your every return, including strokes from the back line and at the net. The drop shot is very useful when returning an overhead clear from backcourt or a drop shot at the net. The sooner you make contact with the shuttle on your return the better. The best shot is always the one that gets back over the net the quickest. Both are designed to make your opponent move or run. If an opponent is unfit, the drop shot will uncover this weakness and exploit it. Drop shots are used to attack the opponent at the four corners of the court and force the return to be lifted, putting you or your team on offense. Patience and accuracy are essential elements of the drop shot.

You can combine the practice for these two strokes into a single session by alternating between the two strokes. This drill incorporates movement and placement that simulate game conditions. Although your partner is stationary near the service line, you will move back and forth between the service line and the back line. You will hit a drop shot from the back line and a hairpin from the service line. Player A initiates the rally with a clear to B. Player B hits an overhead dropshot. Player A returns with a hairpin dropshot at the net (figure 9.5). This will provide you with speed and necessary skill to respond to your opponent's hairpin or long return stroke after your drop shot in a game. Each corner should be covered during a single session.

Overhead Smash

At the moment of impact during a smash, badminton is the fastest racket sport in the world. Initial speeds of over 200 miles per hour have been recorded. Although the overhead jump smash is the most spectacular stroke during any match, a smash does not always result in a point. If you do not time the jump correctly or direct the smash to the right location, you can easily lose balance and give your opponent an easy point. Any smash is an attempt to put away an opponent's return. The smash is most effective when your opponent hits a stroke high and near the middle of the court (figure 9.6). Aim at the middle of your opponent's body. There is nothing like a well-hit smash to boost your confidence and excite the audience during a match.

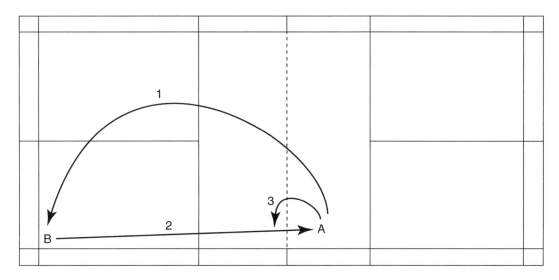

Figure 9.5 Hairpin at the net.

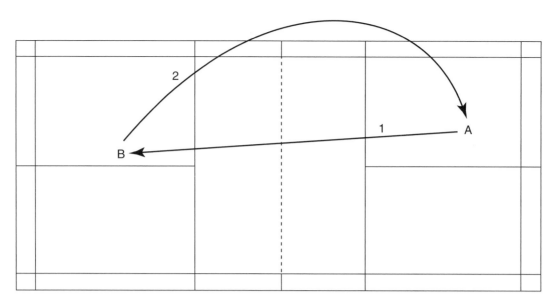

Figure 9.6 Overhead smash with a clear return to the backcourt.

Your partner stands near the short service line and gives you a long, high return near backcourt for you to smash with a full swing. Your partner then returns your smash with another underhand clear. Attempt to repeat this sequence for five consecutive times. Because the smash is more physically demanding than other strokes, limit your practice of the stroke by doing about 15 smashes per side in three repetitions before switching roles with your partner.

Overhead Smash, Hairpin at the Net, and Overhead Drop Shot

Because singles is a running game and relies on a player's ability to sustain a rally, clears, drops, and smashes are essential elements of a successful singles player. Use clears and drop shots to move your opponent around the court. Hit smashes downward with force to put away short clear returns. This running style of play requires stamina and racket control.

You can combine your practice of all three strokes into a single session by alternating among the three strokes. Your partner is stationary near the service line. You will move back and forth between the service line and the back line. Your partner begins the drill with a friendly underhand clear to you in the backcourt. For your first stroke, hit a smash from the back line. Your partner will return your smash with an underhand drop shot. Your second stroke is a hairpin from the service line. Your partner then feeds you a clear from the net to your backcourt. You hit an overhead drop shot for your third shot, followed by another clear from your partner. Repeat this sequence—overhead smash, hairpin drop, overhead drop, hairpin drop—for 10 minutes. This sequence will help with conditioning and footwork and will increase your skill level so you can respond to an opponent's hairpin drop or long return shot during a game. Cover each corner during a single session.

Tactics Drill 3. *Clear–Smash–Block Continuous Rally*

Player A begins the rally with an underhand clear approximately midcourt to player B (figure 9.7). Player B smashes straight ahead at player A, who blocks his or her partner's smash with a drop shot return or returns his or her partner's smash with a clear return. Player B then clears to player A, and they repeat the rally.

Success Check

- Smashes travel downward with some power.
- Block returns stay close to net and fall from lack of power.
- Clear returns are high and deep.

Score Your Success

Rally for 30 seconds or more without missing = 5 points

Rally for 20 to 29 seconds without missing = 3 points

Rally for 10 to 19 seconds without missing = 1 point

Your score ____

Figure 9.7 Clear–smash–block continuous rally drill.

Tactics Drill 4. *Four-Shot Rally*

Player A serves high to player B, who hits a straight-ahead drop shot (figure 9.8). Player C is stationed at the net and returns the drop shot with a hairpin net drop shot. Player D attempts to put this net shot away by hitting it down toward the floor. Player E retrieves and returns the shuttle to player A. Repeat the sequence four times, alternating serves from the right service court to the left service court twice. Then rotate positions. Player A becomes the receiver and player E the server. Player B moves into the net and player C remains at the net but on the opposite side. Player D is now stationed in the backcourt and retrieves the shuttles for player E to serve. Repeat the four-shot rally sequence four times and rotate again.

Success Check

- Use proper footwork.
- Hit clears high and deep.
- Rebound drop shots close to the top of the net.

Score Your Success

Complete three or four rallies without missing = 10 points

Complete two rallies without missing = 5 points

Complete one rally without missing = 1 point

Your score ___

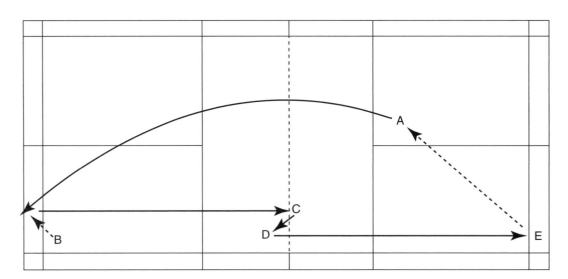

Figure 9.8 Four-shot rally.

Tactics Drill 5. *Wide Doubles Serve–Net Shot Rally*

Player B serves wide and short to player A. Player A returns the serve with a straight-ahead net drop shot to the server's backhand side (figure 9.9). Player B hits a crosscourt drop to player A, who redrops to player C's forehand alley. Player C then crosscourt drops to player A, and the rally continues until one of the three players misses a return. Player B and player C hit only crosscourt drop shots. Player A hits only straight net drop shots.

Success Check

- Serves stay close to top of the net.
- Net drop shot returns travel close to top of the net and fall close to the net.

Score Your Success

Rally for 30 seconds or more without missing = 5 points

Rally for 20 to 29 seconds without missing = 3 points

Rally for 10 to 19 seconds without missing = 1 point

Your score ____

Figure 9.9   Wide doubles serve–net shot rally drill.

Tactics Drill 6. *Flat Drive Continuous Rally*

Player A sets up player B by hitting a drive to him or her near midcourt. Player B hits a forehand or backhand drive back (figure 9.10). The rally continues until one of the players misses. Keep these returns at approximately waist high or higher, with a mixture of forehand and backhand exchanges. Emphasize a quick-quick or flat-flat exchange back and forth over the net.

Success Check

• Drives stay close to top of the net and travel horizontally.

Score Your Success

Rally for 30 seconds or more without missing = 5 points

Rally for 20 to 29 seconds without missing = 3 points

Rally for 10 to 19 seconds without missing = 1 point

Your score ____

Figure 9.10   Flat drive continuous rally drill.

Tactics Drill 7. *Six-Shot Rallies*

These rallies emphasize stroke production, that is, your choice of return from various locations on the court during any rally or point. Use the following six-shot rallies to practice your strokes. You may perform the drills beginning from the right or left side of the court. Where you begin necessarily places more emphasis on the forehand or backhand returns.

Rally 1 (figure 9.11*a*)

1. Straight clear
2. Straight return clear
3. Crosscourt clear
4. Straight return clear
5. Crosscourt drop shot
6. Net drop shot

Rally 2 (figure 9.11*b*)

1. Straight clear
2. Crosscourt drop shot
3. Net drop shot return
4. Crosscourt drive or push
5. Straight clear
6. Crosscourt smash

Rally 3 (figure 9.11*c*)

1. Crosscourt clear
2. Crosscourt smash
3. Net shot
4. Crosscourt clear
5. Straight clear
6. Straight smash

Rally 4 (figure 9.11*d*)

1. Crosscourt clear
2. Crosscourt drop shot
3. Net shot
4. Crosscourt clear
5. Straight smash
6. Crosscourt drive

Success Check

- Hit clears high and deep.
- Hit smashes downward with some pace.
- Let drop shots fall close to the top of the net.
- Hit drive shots quickly and in a flat trajectory.

Score Your Success

Complete three or four rallies without missing = 10 points

Complete two rallies without missing = 5 points

Complete one rally without missing = 1 point

Your score ___

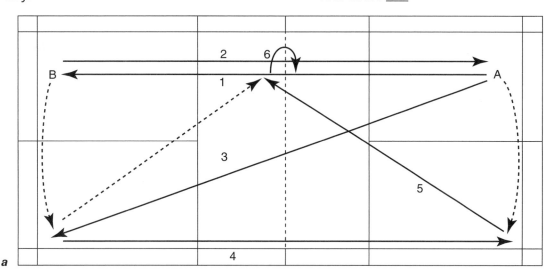

Figure 9.11 Six-shot rallies.

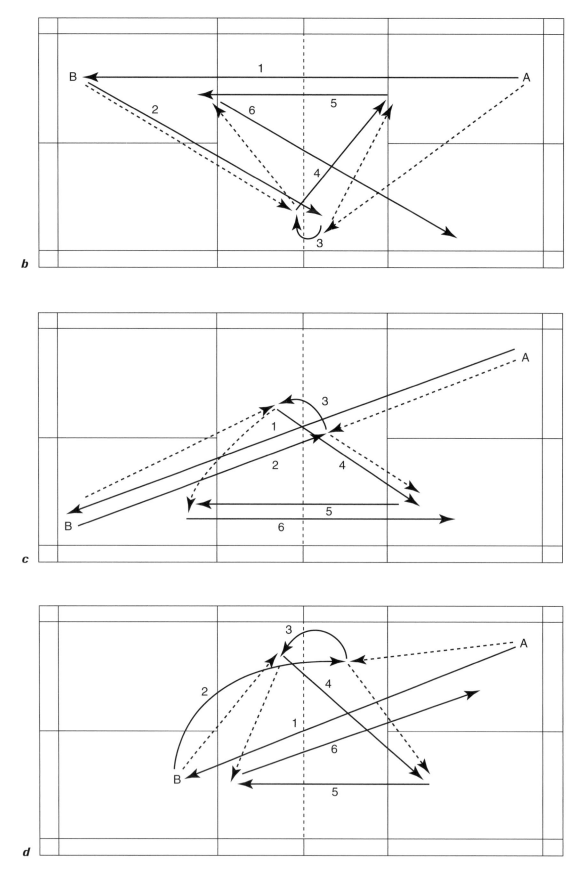

Figure 9.11 (continued).

TIPS FOR SINGLES PLAY

In badminton doubles play, you and your partner must play together in tandem and complement each other in order to be successful. Singles requires you to play by yourself; thus you receive all of the reward and all of the responsibility for success or failure.

Playing singles has many benefits. You become more physically fit and confident in your ability to sustain a lengthy badminton match. Becoming a champion is based on physical conditioning, stroke production, and your ability to adapt to the strengths and weaknesses of your opponents. Whether you win or lose, you must accept the fact that you are the only one responsible for the match. This also means it is very lonely at times because there is no one to discuss your problems with during a match. Recent rule changes in scoring have shortened the time of the match; therefore, you have less time to overcome any early mistakes during a match. The following are suggestions for playing the singles game of badminton:

1. A long, precise service is vital to the start of any point.

2. Always position yourself near the middle of the court after all strokes.

3. The psychological advantage can be lost to your opponent if you display any physical weakness. Remember to keep in mind that even a simple facial expression of discouragement on your part may lead to added encouragement for your opponent.

4. The game is not over until the shuttlecock lands on the court. Keep your eye on the shuttlecock until that very moment and try your best.

5. Use the first few points early in the match to analyze the opponent's weakness and strength. The sooner you can figure out your opponent's weaknesses, your chance of winning increases.

6. Once you have figured out a weakness, continue to exploit the weakness during the match. There is little advantage to playing to your opponent's strength during any match except as a means for exposing a weakness. For example, if an opponent has a weak backhand, you might have to hit to his or her forehand so that you can open up the backhand area.

7. There is a good chance you will be playing against the same player in the future. A well-documented recollection of the match on any particular player will be valuable information for you as you prepare for the next match against the same player.

8. If you do not believe you can win against your opponent, there is no way you can be the winner. Always believe in yourself going into any match and do not lose that confidence until the last point of the match.

You cannot plan a specific strategy for every possible situation. However, there are general principles you can apply to almost every singles game plan or strategy, particularly as your skill level increases:

- Play to your strengths and to your opponent's weaknesses.

- Force your opponent into making errors by being very consistent and steady.

- Keep your opponent moving.

- Change the pace during play.

- Never change a winning strategy; always change a losing strategy.

- Try to make all your overhead strokes look the same; deception is a key part of becoming a better player.

Practice until your singles play results in accurate and successful stroke production. When you are ready, ask a coach or instructor to observe you and check your stroke production during actual singles game play. Attempt to visualize each stroke and critique your shot selection with your evaluator after the match.

Misstep

You fail to make your opponent move and thus give him or her more time with less effort.

Correction

Your every return should have the objective of moving your opponent out of his or her centercourt.

Tactics Drill 8. *Modified Singles*

The playing area of the singles court is reduced as shown in figure 9.12 (shaded areas). Play can begin with any type of serve. All other singles rules apply. Players may use only clears and drop shots to win rallies and points. Keep score as in normal singles play.

Success Check

• Use proper footwork.

• Hit clears high and deep.

• Let drop shots fall close to the top of the net.

Score Your Success

Win the game = 5 points

Your score ___

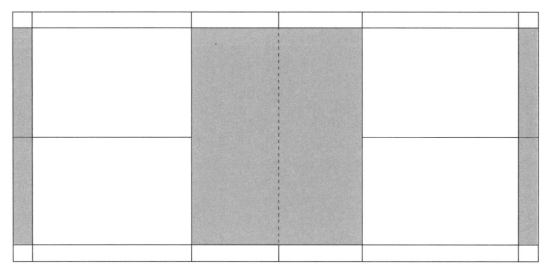

Figure 9.12 Playing area for modified singles.

TIPS FOR DOUBLES PLAY

Playing doubles has similar benefits to singles. You become physically fit and confident in your ability to work together and play as a team. Becoming a champion is based on physical conditioning, stroke production, and your ability to adapt to the strengths and weaknesses of your opponents. Whether you win or lose, you must accept the fact that you and your partner are both responsible for the match. You win together or lose together. This also means that it is very important to discuss any problems and strategy with your partner during a match. Recent rule changes in scoring have shortened the time of the match; therefore, you have less time to overcome any early mistakes during a match. The following are suggestions for playing the doubles game of badminton:

1. A short, precise service is vital to the start of any point.

2. Always position yourself near the middle of the court before serving and receiving as well as after all offensive returns.

3. The server and the receiver are both stationed in an up position near the short service line in the middle of the court. Partners of the server and the receiver are stationed in the back position near midcourt.

4. Any return in doubles that is directed upward requires you and your partner to assume a side-by-side defensive position. You and your partner will rotate between these two positions depending on which type of return you make.

5. The psychological advantage can be lost to your opponents if you or your partner display any physical weakness. Remember to keep in mind that even a simple facial expression of discouragement on your part may lead to added encouragement for your opponents. If one partner appears to show some discomfort, make the majority of your returns to that person.

6. The game is not over until the shuttlecock lands on the court. Keep your eye on the shuttlecock until that very moment and try your best.

7. Use the first few points early in the match to analyze the opposing team's weaknesses and strengths. Always play the majority of your returns to the weaker of the two opponents. The sooner you can figure out your opponents' weaknesses, your chance of winning increases.

8. Once you have figured out a weakness, continue to exploit the weakness during the match. There is little advantage to playing to your opponents' strengths during any match except as a means for exposing a weakness. For example, if an opponent has a weak backhand, you might have to hit to his or her forehand so that you can open up the backhand area.

9. There is a good chance you will be playing against the same team in the future. A well-documented recollection of the match on any particular doubles team will be valuable information for you as you prepare for the next match against the same team.

10. If you do not believe you can win against your opponents, there is little chance you will win. Always believe you can win any match and do not lose that confidence until the last point of the match.

SUCCESS SUMMARY OF TACTICS AND STRATEGIES

Tactics or strategy for singles and doubles are deliberate efforts by you or your opponent to win points and regain serve. Effective strategy plays to your strengths and away from your opponent's strengths, if possible. If your opponent lacks conditioning, attempt to make him or her run to tire him or her out. Because most players do not have as strong a backhand as they do a forehand, hit the majority of your shots to the backhand. Vary your returns to keep your opponent off balance. If you are not very fit, try to attack quickly and make your rallies as short as possible by smashing or hitting outright winners. You should be less aggressive on your serve and play safer, more conservative returns on your opponent's serve. Also, learn the singles and doubles boundaries really well so as not to play any of your opponent's returns that would have been out. Players who cooperate and complement each other will become a more successful doubles team. Good doubles players trust each other and continually strive to be in the correct position and make the best returns during doubles play. They create a level of trust by playing the same style of play no matter their partner. Because they are predictable and consistent, they are easy to play with and fun to have as a partner.

Tactics Drills

1. Short Serve–Push Return	___ out of 10
2. Short Serve–Net Drop Shot	___ out of 10
3. Clear–Smash–Block Continuous Rally	___ out of 5
4. Four-Shot Rally	___ out of 10
5. Wide Doubles Serve–Net Shot Rally	___ out of 5
6. Flat Drive Continuous Rally	___ out of 5
7. Six-Shot Rallies	___ out of 10
8. Modified Singles	___ out of 5
Total	**___ out of 60**

If you scored at least 45 out of a possible 60 points, you are ready to move on to the next step. If you scored fewer than 45 points, repeat the drills that were difficult for you. Have a coach, instructor, or experienced player evaluate your skill.

Doubles play is the next step. Doubles play is less demanding than singles play, especially at the recreational level. However, strength, endurance, speed, eye–hand coordination, and aerobic conditioning are necessary for both. (Conditioning will be covered in step 11.) Doubles also requires cooperative play and teamwork. You either win together or lose together. Players learn to complement each other and work in tandem. Similar to singles, badminton doubles is a game that you can play throughout your life.

Doubles Play

Doubles play is very different from singles, primarily because you now have a partner, but also because you usually have less time to think and react. Doubles tactics are greatly dependent upon court position. You will probably enjoy doubles play and have more success if you learn to rotate and play as a team. The rotational system consists of you and your partner rotating from an up-and-back position to a side-by-side position, depending on whether you are on offense or defense. The team on offense has the shuttle directed downward, and they will change to a side-by-side or defending position when either partner is forced to hit the shuttle upward.

Starting in and maintaining the correct court position are essential to successful doubles play. An important element of this principle involves trusting your partner during the rally. Allow your partner to make his or her own shots. Hit serves and returns during any doubles rally with the objective of forcing your opponents to lift to you or your partner.

Men's, women's, and mixed doubles require the same strokes, techniques, teamwork, and strategy to be successful. In normal doubles play, both the server and the receiver play close to the net and their partners are temporarily responsible for the backcourt. The initial stroke by either team is meant to maneuver their opponents into a position that requires them to lift their returns. The subsequent misdirection or jockeying for the offensive position usually determines which team wins the rally.

Doubles play in badminton is enjoyable for many reasons. It is a great recreational game that you can enjoy socially and competitively. It allows you to practice teamwork and strategy. Doubles play also gets your heart beating faster, requires that you move quickly, and makes you think on your feet. This mental practice and physical activity possibly aid in allowing you to relax, relieving stress, and providing some physical conditioning. Step 11 suggests several exercises and drills to develop your physical conditioning for badminton play. Doubles play is less demanding than singles play, especially at the recreational level, but strength, endurance, speed, eye–hand coordination, and aerobic conditioning are necessary for both. Doubles also requires cooperative play and teamwork. You either win together or lose together. Similar to singles, badminton doubles is a game you can play throughout your life.

COURT POSITIONING FOR DOUBLES

Your position in doubles to a great extent determines the type of return that you or your partner will make and how effectively you will both be able to get to your opponents' return. Figure 10.1 shows the beginning position for both teams as the serve is delivered. Both the server and the receiver are trying to get their opponents to lift the shuttle up to them or to their partners. Initially, both teams are vying for the offensive position, so they both start up and back. Because you can score on every point, it is necessary to develop an accurate and consistent low serve while standing as close to the short service line and the centerline as possible. Errors on the serve now result in a point for the receiving team so consistency and accuracy are of even more importance while serving. Errors on the serve must be eliminated as much as possible. With the new rally scoring system, the server is not rewarded for aggressive or risky maneuvers. The drive and flick serves may give your opponents a different look and keep them more honest while they are receiving the serve. You can use either the forehand or backhand serving motion effectively. Because the low serve is used most often, it is important to hit a safe, conservative return of serve that will keep your opponents honest and cause them to lift your return. The new scoring system does not seem to reward riskier returns of serve that result in unforced errors or have little chance for success.

Figure 10.1 Beginning positions for doubles players. Both teams begin play in up and back positions.

Misstep

You consistently serve the shuttle too short or too high.

Correction

This error can lead you to lack confidence in the short serve, leading to a lack of success. Practice the short serve with both forehand and backhand deliveries until you are consistent and confident.

One of the following three returns should be successful: a push shot, a midcourt drive, or a net drop shot. Direct the midcourt drive or push shot past the partner at the net to cause the back partner to contact the shuttle low and force him or her to lift the shuttle upward. However, if the partner who is up does not play aggressively toward the net after serving, then a hairpin or tumble drop shot at the net should force him or her to hit the shuttle up. The half-court drive or push return is your best overall answer to a good serve. Half-court returns and drives are the safest choices during men's, women's, and mixed doubles play. The main objectives are to keep the shuttle going downward, gain the offensive position, and keep it. Figures 10.2 and 10.3 illustrate the rotational system of doubles court coverage.

Figure 10.2 Doubles positions using an up-and-back offense and defense after a service return.

Misstep

You and your partner have indecision about who should make the return.

Correction

Try to consistently be in the proper position. When returns are hit down the middle of the court, the partner who has the shuttle on his or her forehand side should make the return.

Figure 10.3 Doubles positions during a rally using an up-and-back offense and a side-by-side defense.

The up-and-back system is preferable when you have the shuttle going down into your opponents' court or when your opponents are forced to hit upward. The side-by-side formation provides a better defense and allows you and your partner to more easily return any of your opponents' shots that are hit downward. Gener-ally speaking, every return you or your partner make should have the objective of forcing your opponents to lift or clear their return. However, the rotational system, in which you change from being up and back to being side by side, allows transition between offensive and defensive rallies.

Misstep

Too many of your returns are hit upward.

Correction

When in doubt, smash!

At times you or your partner will have to lift or clear the shuttle. In this case, you should shift to the side-by-side formation. If you or your partner is able to hit a return downward and force your opponents to lift the shuttle, then you should shift into the up-and-back formation.

Another example of shifting to the up-and-back formation would be on a high serve delivered to you or your partner. As soon as the high serve is delivered to your partner, change places. From his or her up position receiving the serve, he or she moves back to return the high serve. From your back position straddling the centerline, move to the net and prepare for any net returns from your partner's downward return of serve. The same is true in reverse when either you or your partner initiates a high serve. When a high serve is delivered from the server's up position, he or she rotates back into the side-by-side formation. As soon as you recognize your partner's high serve, you move opposite your partner, side by side, to cover the other side.

PLAYING AS A TEAM

Communication is important between partners, before, during, and after the game. Partners should complement each other. You should work in tandem in order to be successful both offensively and defensively. Remember, you win together or lose together. Your actions determine the outcome for the team, success or failure. Short, distinct verbal cues to your partner, such as, "Out!" during a rally, may assist your partner. Verbal commands such as "Take it!" or "Yours!" may help your partner on returns that are not clearly defined as to who should make the potential return. Two key elements must be accomplished if you and your partner are to be successful in doubles play:

1. The server must develop the confidence and ability to deliver a short serve successfully.

2. The server must play aggressively toward the net after the delivery of the serve in order to prevent the opponent from returning the serve with a drop shot.

Trusting your partner plays a significant role in the success of a doubles team. If you or your partner consistently fool each other or do not do what the other partner expects, there will be an element of confusion, which may lead to mistrust of each other. This lack of trust may lead to a point where it is not fun to play doubles together. At that point in time, criticism may not be well received, no matter how accurate or pertinent it is.

Misstep

Partners do not cooperate or try to complement each other's strengths and weaknesses.

Correction

Work together. Discuss strategy, strengths, weaknesses, and court coverage with your partner before play.

Misstep

You lack communication during play.

Correction

Discuss specific game situations before playing.

Other general strategies for doubles play are:

- Always try to hit returns downward to your opponents, which will require them to lift their returns. Even if your returns lack speed, such as fast drops or half smashes, your opponents will be required to hit their returns up to you or your partner. This will allow you and your partner to remain in the up-and-back positions and stay on the offensive.

- When serving, serve the low, short serve most of the time. Because of the new scoring system, there is no room for unforced errors on the serve.

- When serving, play aggressively toward the net. Absolutely prevent your opponents from hitting drop shots.

- When receiving, get as close as possible to the net, but always be thinking "long serve." Push or misdirect most returns past the up opponent.

- When smashing, smash straight ahead most of the time.

- Get the shuttle over the net as soon as possible. A straight net drop shot is usually preferable to one hit crosscourt, unless your opponent is directly in front of you across the net. The best return is the one that gets over the net the quickest. The less time your opponent has, the better.

Misstep

Your returns give you less time and your opponent more time to respond or recover.

Correction

Develop a proper strategy. Cooperate and communicate. Help each other by calling out birds during rallies and on short or long serves. Play the bird to the weaker of the two opponents. Slow drop shots or clears are the least attractive returns.

In doubles play, it is much more difficult to hit the shuttle away from both of your opponents. If you hit it away from one partner, you are essentially hitting it to the other. You must be able to serve low and short to your opponents successfully. Never attempt to direct the shuttle upward during a rally. Partners trying to cover too much court or trying to make all the shots may create problems. Avoid criticizing or blaming your partner for mistakes or missed shots.

Doubles Drill 1. *Wide Doubles Short Serve Drill*

Player A serves wide and short to player B. Player B returns this forehand short serve with a straight-ahead drop shot at the net to his or her partner's forehand and backhand side alleys. This is not a rally. Player A serves until player B accomplishes five good returns toward his or her forehand. Then repeat to his or her backhand side alley. These drop shot returns should carry into his or her partner's backhand side alley and short of the short service line to be considered good returns. After five good returns of each have been made, players reverse roles and repeat the process. Repeat drill using the short backhand serve.

Success Check

- Serves cross over close to the top of net.
- Serves travel crosscourt and toward the alley.
- Drop shot returns travel close to the net and fall toward the floor.

Score Your Success

Complete 20 good drop shot returns from forehand serve = 5 points

Complete 20 good drop shot returns from backhand serve = 5 points

Your score ___

Doubles Drill 2. *High Serve–Rotate–Smash–Block*

Doubles teams A and B are on opposite sides of the net in up and back positions (figure 10.4). Player B1 starts in up position to receive the serve. Player A1 serves a high flick or drive serve high to player B1. Players A1 and A2 fall into a side-by-side defensive position. Players B1 and B2 change positions. As player B1 retreats to hit the high serve, player B2 goes to the net. Player B1 hits a smash return and either A1 or A2 attempts to return the smash with a block.

To Increase Difficulty

- Serving team attempts to clear the smash return instead of blocking it.
- Server may use flick or drive serve to increase difficulty for the receiver.

Success Check

- Serving team moves into side-by-side defensive position.
- Receiving team switches positions to retain up-and-back offensive position.

Score Your Success

Complete five good sequences without a miss = 10 points

Complete three or four good sequences without a miss = 5 points

Complete one or two good sequences without a miss = 1 point

Your score ___

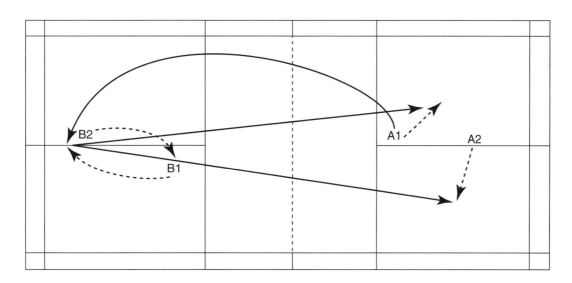

Figure 10.4 High serve–rotate–smash–block.

Doubles Drill 3. *Short Serve–Push Return Rally*

Player A1 must initiate the serve from within the service court. Player A1 serves short to player B1 (figure 10.5). Player B1 returns this short serve with a push return to his or her opponent's backhand side alley or a push return to his or her opponent's forehand side alley. This is a rally, therefore player A2 should attempt to return this shot with a push return to player B2 near midcourt. These pushed midcourt drive returns should carry beyond each partner's short service line and be directed near the opponent's side alley. Players A1 and B1 should remain near the T area and feint as if trying to intercept the returns being made down the sidelines. Alternate serving from both the right and left service courts. After players A2 and B2 have made an exchange of at least five good returns from each service court, both sets of partners switch places. Player A2 should serve short to player B2 and allow him or her to make five good push returns of serve. Players A1 and B1 attempt to rally back and forth down the sidelines.

Success Check

- Serves stay close to top of the net.
- Push returns travel close to top of the net and fall near midcourt.

Score Your Success

Rally for five returns or more from each service court without missing = 10 points

Rally for three or four returns from each service court without missing = 5 points

Rally for one or two returns from each service court without missing = 1 point

Your score ___

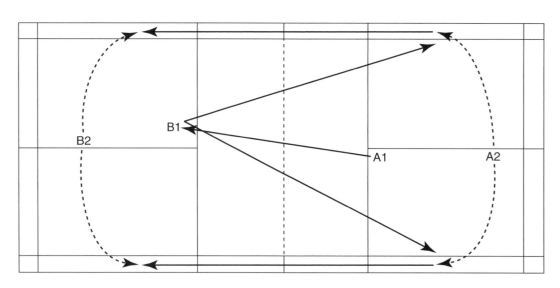

Figure 10.5 Short serve–push return rally.

Doubles Drill 4. *Modified Doubles*

The playing area of the doubles court is reduced to the areas shown in figure 10.6. Players may use any type of return or shot to win rallies and points. However, after the initial doubles serve, only the side alleys are inbounds. Otherwise, keep your score just as in normal doubles play.

Success Check

- Use proper footwork.
- Cover the court with proper formation.
- Direct most shots downward or make them fall close to the top of the net.

Score Your Success

Win the game = 10 points

Lose the game = 5 points

Your score ___

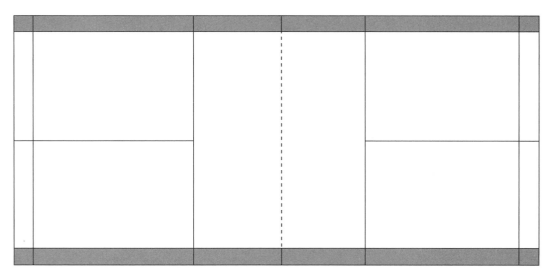

Figure 10.6 Court boundaries for modified doubles.

Doubles Drill 5. *Clear–Smash–No Drops Doubles*

The playing area of the doubles court is reduced as shown in figure 10.6 (shaded areas). Play can begin with any type of serve. All other doubles rules apply. Players may use only clears and smashes, not drop shots, to win rallies and points. Keep score as in normal doubles play.

Success Check

- Use proper footwork.
- Hit clears high and deep.
- Smashes, half smashes, and fast drops should land past short service lines.

Score Your Success

Win the game = 10 points

Score 15 to 20 points = 5 points

Score 10 to 14 points = 1 point

Your score ___

Doubles Drill 6. *Mini-Minton*

Player A serves short to player B. Player B returns this short serve with a push return or a drop shot to player A's backhand or forehand side. This is a game played at the net using rally scoring. Therefore, both players should attempt to return this shot without hitting their return past the short service line. Any returns that carry beyond the short service line are out and the other player scores a point. Players A and B should remain near the T area and feint as if trying to intercept the returns being made down the sidelines. Play continues with rally scoring until someone scores 21 points to win the game.

Success Check

- Serves stay close to top of the net.
- Push and drop shot returns travel close to top of the net and fall short of the short service line.

Score Your Success

Win the game = 10 points

Lose the game = 5 points

Your score ____

Doubles Drill 7. *Net Put-Away*

Stand at the T or frontcourt position for doubles play. Five shuttles are affixed to the top of the net at about 3-foot intervals. Each shuttle is pushed down on the net; use the feathers to attach the shuttles to the net. One shuttle is placed in the middle of the net with the other four placed two each on either side. Rush the net and simulate putting a shuttle away as if it were being dropped from the opponent's side of the net. The racket must be swung in a horizontal path relative to the net and must not contact the net. Each shuttle is hit or brushed with a flat racket. After each hit, return quickly to the T position and then quickly rush the net and attempt to put the next shuttle in line away. Continue until all of the shuttles have been hit.

Success Check

- Hit returns downward.
- The racket does not contact the net.
- Shuttles fall immediately to the floor on the opponent's side.

Score Your Success

Hit all five shuttles successfully = 10 points

Hit three or four shuttles successfully = 5 points

Hit one or two shuttles successfully = 1 point

Your score ____

Doubles Drill 8. *Triangle Doubles*

This is a drill played to 30 points using rally scoring. Three players are stationed on each side of the net. On each side, one player is in the up position near the T and the two other players are stationed in backcourt. Each player is responsible for half of the backcourt. Players A1 and B1 stand at the T or frontcourt position for doubles play.

Either player A1 or B1 begins play by delivering a short serve. Following the return of serve, play continues until an error is made. Accurate serves and service returns are important, and any returns that are lifted almost always will be smashed. This places a premium on defense, placement, and an attacking style of play. All players on both sides play their positions until one team scores 10 points. Then each team rotates clockwise. Players A1 and B1 rotate back to the right side of the backcourt. Players A2 and B2 rotate from backcourt right to backcourt left. Players A3 and B3 rotate forward and play the up positions. All players on either side play their positions until one team scores 20 points. Then teams rotate clockwise again. Players A1 and B1 rotate to the left backcourt, players A3 and B3 move to the right backcourt, and players A2 and B2 are the net players until the end of the game. The first team to 30 points wins the game.

Success Check

- Hit returns downward. Fast drops or smashes are the best choices.

- Slow returns are least attractive and most often will be put away by the net player.

Score Your Success

Winning team = 10 points

First team to 20 points = 5 points

First team to 10 points = 5 points

Your score ____

SUCCESS SUMMARY OF DOUBLES PLAY

Starting in and maintaining the correct court position are essential to successful doubles play. An important element of this principle involves trusting your partner during the rally. Allow your partner to make his or her own shots. Hit serves and returns during any doubles rally with the objective of forcing your opponents to lift the shuttle to you or your partner. Men's, women's, and mixed doubles require the same strokes, techniques, teamwork, and strategy to be successful. In normal doubles play, both the server and the receiver play close to the net and their partners are temporarily responsible for the backcourt. The initial stroke by either team is intended to maneuver the other team into a position that requires them to lift the return. The subsequent misdirection or jockeying for the offensive position usually determines which team wins the rally.

Record your drill scores and note your total for this step.

Doubles Drills

1. Wide Doubles Short Serve Drill	___ out of 10
2. High Serve–Rotate–Smash–Block	___ out of 10
3. Short Serve–Push Return Rally	___ out of 10
4. Modified Doubles	___ out of 10
5. Clear–Smash–No Drops Doubles	___ out of 10
6. Mini-Minton	___ out of 10
7. Net Put-Away	___ out of 10
8. Triangle Doubles	___ out of 20
Total	___ *out of 90*

If you scored at least 70 out of a possible 90 points, you have mastered the skills required for solid doubles play. If you scored fewer than 70 points, repeat the drills that were difficult for you. Have a coach, instructor, or experienced player evaluate your skill.

The last step covers the topic of conditioning. Good conditioning is especially important in singles play. Train for muscular strength and endurance, aerobic and anaerobic fitness, and flexibility to maximize your performance on the court and improve your overall fitness.

Conditioning

Singles play is generally a game of fitness and patience. You are responsible for your good and bad shots. The primary objective of the beginning singles player is to keep the rally going. A beginning player will most often hit clears and drop shots to accomplish this task. Your success or failure usually depends on your ability to sustain the rally and maneuver your opponent around the court until he or she hits a weak return. However, the ultimate objective should always be to win the rally and score points. Advanced badminton players add the smash, drive, and around-the-head shots, along with variation and greater skill in execution. They learn to sustain the rally even with better players and dictate their opponent's return to a great extent.

Changes in the pace and the location of the serve are also important. Develop your skill in executing the attacking clear, fast drop shot, and half smash if the situation requires it. The quality of your strokes and your ability to execute them under pressure during game play determine whether you win or lose. Accuracy and deception in shot making, along with good reflexes and endurance, greatly increase your ability to cover the court in singles play.

Singles play in badminton provides the opportunity to succeed or fail in competition on your terms. Badminton singles is also an excellent form of aerobic exercise and is beneficial in improving your cardiovascular conditioning and overall health. Other rewards exist in the forms of recreational, social, and psychological benefits, as well as tangible awards, such as trophies, medals, rankings, and so forth.

COMPONENTS OF FITNESS

A badminton player can become a better competitor by being more physically fit. In close matches, fitness usually is a factor in the outcome. The most important considerations in a badminton-conditioning program are muscular strength, muscular endurance, aerobic training (cardiovascular endurance), anaerobic training (interval, circuit, and overspeed training), flexibility, concentration (mental practice), and prevention of injuries.

Material in the Conditioning section based on material previously published in "Common Injuries in Badminton," by Tony Grice, *Badminton Magazine*, vol. 3, no. 2, April 1988, and in *Badminton* (4th ed.) by Tony Grice, 1996, Boston, American Press.

Along with the physical exercises to develop these factors, make sure to include a sound diet, adequate sleep and rest, and acceptable training rules. The following sections describe specific conditioning exercises to develop these areas of fitness.

Muscular Strength and Muscular Endurance

Training with weights is an excellent method of developing muscular strength and muscular endurance. Research indicates that a moderate weight-training program using resistance at approximately 50 to 60 percent of maximal strength with 8 to 12 repetitions will develop both muscular strength and muscular endurance. In the section on circuit training, the sample programs include strength training. Push-ups and volleying against a backboard with a covered racket will increase wrist, arm, and shoulder strength and endurance. Sit-ups or curl-ups aid in developing abdominal strength and endurance. Rope jumping improves footwork and increases leg strength and endurance.

Aerobic Training or Cardiovascular Endurance

Running is valuable for muscular and cardiorespiratory endurance. Jogging or distance running, running up and down steps, and rope jumping are all excellent conditioners for aerobic training. Extremely long-distance running is probably not necessary for badminton players. A moderately fast pace for 2 to 4 miles (3.2 to 6.4 km) will yield better results than a 10-mile (16.1 km) run at a very slow pace. A minimum of three days of aerobic training per week is recommended; five to seven days per week are recommended for the advanced or elite badminton player. The individual skill level is the primary factor used to identify the aerobic training program needed. Before a competition or tournament, a tapering program several days beforehand will also be required. Two or three days of moderate exercise with no intense training is recommended for adequate recovery and the replacement of energy stores before a big event.

Anaerobic Training

Anaerobic training can be accomplished in a number of ways. The ability to change direction quickly is essential in the fast-paced game of badminton. Short sprints and shuttle runs requiring a reach, touch, and change of direction are very good for improving speed of movement. A recent study determined that during a badminton match, the shuttle is actually in play approximately 50 percent of the time. This indicates that badminton is an intermittent activity with short bursts of activity followed by periods of inactivity, such as walking around, taking deep breaths, and changing courts. Even though play is supposed to be continuous, there is a lot of inactivity between points.

Interval training duplicates this type of discontinuous activity. Interval training usually involves running intervals with fast runs or sprints followed by periods of relief or rest. Most research indicates these intervals are best accomplished with a ratio of 1:2, work versus rest. In other words, run a minute and then rest two. Other forms of interval training might involve uphill running, downhill running, or running steps (bleachers or stairwell). Another example pertains to running laps around an oval track, in which one might run or sprint the straight-aways and walk or jog the curves.

Tables 11.1, 11.2, and 11.3 outline three treadmill workouts that use anaerobic interval training. Before beginning the anaerobic interval training program on the treadmill, warm up and stretch for 5 to 10 minutes. Perform calisthenics along with active and passive stretching to warm up the body and prevent injury. Record your training heart rate at the beginning of each exercise bout, at the end of each bout within 15 seconds after, and approximately 30 seconds before beginning the next bout. Your heart rate should recover or come down to approximately 100 beats per minute (bpm) or less at the end of each rest period and prior to the next exercise bout. If your recovery heart rate remains above 120 bpm following the 2-minute rest period, take a slightly longer rest period of 2.5 to 3 minutes.

Table 11. 1   Treadmill Workout for Well-Conditioned Female and Moderately Conditioned Male Athletes

Activity	Duration	Speed	Rest interval
Walk	3 minutes	3.0 mph (4.8 km/h)	None
Run	7-minute mile (1.6 km)	8.5 mph (13.7 km/h)	2 minutes
Run	3.5-minute half mile (0.8 km)	8.5 mph (13.7 km/h)	2 minutes
Run	1 minute	9.0 mph (14.5 km/h)	2 minutes
Run	1 minute	9.0 mph (14.5 km/h)	2 minutes
Run	1 minute	9.0 mph (14.5 km/h)	2 minutes
Run	1 minute	10.0 mph (16.1 km/h)	2 minutes
Run	1 minute	10.0 mph (16.1 km/h)	2 minutes
Run	1 minute	10.0 mph (16.1 km/h)	2 minutes
Run	1 minute	11.0 mph (17.7 km/h)	2 minutes
Run	1 minute	11.0 mph (17.7 km/h)	2 minutes
Run	1 minute	11.0 mph (17.7 km/h)	2 minutes
Run*	1 minute	12.0 mph (19.3 km/h)	2 minutes
Run*	1 minute	12.0 mph (19.3 km/h)	2 minutes
Run*	1 minute	12.0 mph (19.3 km/h)	2 minutes

<tfn>* The last three runs (1 minute at 12.0 mph [19.3 km/h])are optional or may be added as your fitness level increases.

Table 11. 2   Treadmill Workout for Highly-Conditioned Female and Well-Conditioned Male Athletes

Activity	Duration	Speed	Rest interval
Walk	3 minutes	3.0 mph (4.8 km/h)	None
Run	7-minute mile (1.6 km)	8.5 mph (13.7 km/h)	2 minutes
Run	3.5-minute half mile (0.8 km)	8.5 mph (13.7 km/h)	2 minutes
Run	1 minute	9.0 mph (14.5 km/h)	2 minutes
Run	1 minute	9.0 mph (14.5 km/h)	2 minutes
Run	1 minute	9.0 mph (14.5 km/h)	2 minutes
Run	1 minute	10.0 mph (16.1 km/h)	2 minutes
Run	1 minute	10.0 mph (16.1 km/h)	2 minutes
Run	1 minute	10.0 mph (16.1 km/h)	2 minutes
Run	1 minute	11.0 mph (17.7 km/h)	2 minutes
Run	1 minute	11.0 mph (17.7 km/h)	2 minutes
Run	1 minute	11.0 mph (17.7 km/h)	2 minutes
Run*	1 minute	12.0 mph (19.3 km/h)	2 minutes
Run*	1 minute	12.0 mph (19.3 km/h)	2 minutes
Run*	1 minute	12.0 mph (19.3 km/h)	2 minutes

* The last three runs (1 minute at 12.0 mph [19.3 km/h])are optional or may be added as your fitness level increases.

Table 11.3 Treadmill Workout for Extremely Well-Conditioned Female Elite Athletes and Highly Conditioned Male Athletes

Activity	Duration	Speed	Rest interval
Walk	3 minutes	3.0 mph (4.8 km/h)	None
Run	5.5-minute mile (1.6 km)	11.0 mph (17.7 km/h)	2 minutes
Run	2.75-minute half mile (0.8 km)	11.0 mph (17.7 km/h)	2 minutes
Run	1 minute	12.0 mph (19.3 km/h)	2 minutes
Run	1 minute	12.0 mph (19.3 km/h)	2 minutes
Run	1 minute	12.0 mph (19.3 km/h)	2 minutes
Run	1 minute	13.0 mph (20.1 km/h)	2 minutes
Run	1 minute	13.0 mph (20.1 km/h)	2 minutes
Run	1 minute	13.0 mph (20.1 km/h)	2 minutes
Run	1 minute	14.0 mph (22.4 km/h)	2 minutes
Run	1 minute	14.0 mph (22.4 km/h)	2 minutes
Run	1 minute	14.0 mph (22.4 km/h)	2 minutes
Run*	1 minute	15.0 mph (24.1 km/h)	2 minutes
Run*	1 minute	15.0 mph (24.1 km/h)	2 minutes
Run*	1 minute	15.0 mph (24.1 km/h)	2 minutes

* The last three runs (1 minute at 15.0 mph [24.1 km/h]) are optional or may be added as your fitness level increases.

The entire running program is performed at 0 degrees elevation unless the treadmill has a limit on its maximum speed. If the treadmill cannot go more than 10 miles per hour (16.1 km/h), leave the speed at 10 miles per hour and increase the elevation by 1 degree for each suggested increase in speed beyond 10 miles per hour. For example, the interval at 11 miles per hour (17.7 km/h) would be performed at 10 miles per hour but at 1 degree of elevation. The 12-mile-per-hour (19.3 km/h) intervals would be performed at 10 miles per hour but at 2 degrees of elevation. For rest intervals, reduce the speed of the treadmill to 3.0 miles per hour (4.8 km/h) and walk for the duration of the rest interval.

These treadmill programs are for well-conditioned athletes. The beginning badminton player may be interested in playing at the recreational level only. Therefore, no minimum level of conditioning would be needed in order to play recreationally. But if you are interested in advancing beyond the level of recreational player, you must be able to run or jog a mile in 10 minutes or less. See table 11.4 for sample training programs for beginning, intermediate, and advanced badminton players.

Each of the suggested programs should be followed by at least a 5-minute cool-down walk on the treadmill at 3 miles per hour (4.8 km/h) and 0 elevation. Your heart rate should be down to approximately 90 beats per minute or less at the end of the cool-down period.

Circuit training involves a series of exercises or stations, each one working a specific part of the body spread out over a course or circuit. At each station, the athlete performs a given exercise, then walks, jogs, or runs to the next station, where another exercise is performed. The objective is to complete the circuit in a set time (target time) or work for a specific time period at each station (30 seconds, for example). Another consideration is to have several levels of exercises at each station. When the athlete completes the circuit on the first level under the target time, he or she advances to the next level, which may simply be an increased number of repetitions. The target time remains the same. A circuit-training program potentially

Table 11.4 Sample Circuit-Training Programs for Beginner, Intermediate, and Advanced Players

	Beginner: three days per week	Intermediate: four or five days per week	Advanced: six or seven days per week
Calisthenics	Perform the following: • 10 side-straddle hops or jumping jacks • 25 bent-knee curl-ups • 10 opposite toe touches • 10 push-ups	Perform the following: • 15 side-straddle hops or jumping jacks • 50 bent-knee curl-ups • 15 opposite toe touches • 15 push-ups	Perform the following: • 25 side-straddle hops or jumping jacks • 100 bent-knee curl-ups • 25 opposite toe touches • 25 push-ups
Aerobic	• Walk or jog continuously from .5 to 1.0 mile (.8-1.6 km) at an 8- to 10-minute-mile pace • Perform 100 rope jumps continuously or in 2 sets of 50 repetitions each	• Jog or run continuously for 1 to 3 miles (1.6-4.8 km) at a 7.5- to 8-minute-mile pace • Perform 250 rope jumps continuously or in 5 sets of 50 repetitions each	• Run continuously for 3 to 5 miles (4.8-8.0 km) at a 6- to 7-minute-mile pace • Perform 500 rope jumps continuously or in 5 sets of 100 repetitions each
Anaerobic	• Perform 1 minute of continuous hitting against a flat wall (wall rally) × 5 sets for a total of 5 minutes • Run five 25-yard sprints or 10 shuttle runs the length of the court • Shuffle or slide from sideline to sideline 20 times, touching the doubles sideline with the outside hand each time (can be done in 2 sets of 10 repetitions each)	• Perform 1 minute of continuous wall rally × 10 sets for a total of 10 minutes • Run five 50-yard sprints or 15 shuttle runs the length of the court • Shuffle or slide from sideline to sideline 30 times, touching the doubles sideline with the outside hand each time (can be done in 3 sets of 10 repetitions each)	• Perform 1 minute of continuous wall rally × 15 sets for a total of 15 minutes • Run ten 50-yard sprints or 15 shuttle runs the length of the court • Shuffle or slide from sideline to sideline 50 times, touching the doubles sideline with the outside hand each time (can be done in 5 sets of 10 repetitions each)
Weight training	Perform the following at 50 percent of maximal strength for 8 to 12 repetitions: • Triceps extension • Bench press • Biceps curl • Lateral arm lift • Squat • Leg or knee extension • Wrist roll • Rat curl	Perform the following at 60 percent of maximal strength for 8 to 12 repetitions: • Triceps extension • Bench press • Biceps curl • Lateral arm lift • Squat • Leg or knee extension • Wrist roll • Rat curl	Perform the following at 70 percent of maximal strength for 8 to 12 repetitions: • Triceps extension • Bench press • Biceps curl • Lateral arm lift • Squat • Leg or knee extension • Wrist roll • Rat curl

offers a combination of strength, endurance, flexibility, agility, and cardiorespiratory endurance. Table 11.4 describes three sample circuit training programs for beginning, intermediate, and advanced badminton players who do not have access to a treadmill. They each include an optional weight-training program as well.

Overspeed training deals with the principle of overload in the area of speed training. This type of training requires someone to go faster than he or she normally can. An excellent way to accomplish this is with a motorized treadmill; set the pace faster than you normally can run. For example, you might not be able to run a 4-minute mile, but you can probably run a 4-minute-mile pace for 30 seconds or possibly 1 minute. Increasing the elevation of the treadmill requires you to exaggerate your knee lift to generate more power. Swinging a tennis racket or swinging a badminton racket underwater also provides overspeed training and uses the training principle of *specificity,* which involves training with skills that occur in your chosen sport. Downhill and uphill running are forms of overspeed training.

Plyometrics training also emphasizes overspeed work. Plyometrics training involves bounding, jumping, depth jumping (jumping from a height and rebounding back up into the air or to a new height), and rope jumping. Using heavy ropes or doing double jumps are forms of *overload* or *overspeed* training that emphasize jumping for leg power.

Flexibility

Flexibility refers to the range of motion around the joint. The goal of any stretching activity is to increase muscle flexibility around joints. Almost all types of stretching activities improve flexibility around the major joints at least temporarily.

Some research studies indicate that static, or passive, stretching is less likely to cause injury than active, or ballistic, stretching. A static stretch is one in which you stretch to the farthest position and hold the position, usually for 30 to 40 seconds. During an active stretch, you move or bounce slightly to increase the stretch. The exercises described later in this section are examples of static stretches. Jumping jacks and opposite toe touches are examples of active stretches. A stretching method called proprioceptive neuromuscular facilitation (PNF) utilizes a partner who assists by briefly resisting against the contraction of the muscle group being stretched. After the muscle relaxes, the partner passively stretches the muscle beyond its normal range of motion. PNF stretching should be done only under the supervision of a trained professional. Recreational or amateur players who are unfamiliar with the stretching technique could easily overstretch and strain their muscles.

Stretching increases flexibility but does not seem to improve strength or performance. Recent research suggests that athletes benefit more by improving their fitness levels along with increasing flexibility. A common assumption is that improved flexibility helps to prevent injuries. However poor aerobic fitness is more highly correlated with the risk of significant injury than poor flexibility.

The badminton athlete should integrate stretching into a warm-up program that also includes aerobic activity. It is recommended that stretching be done after aerobic activity. Warm muscles stretch more easily and remain stretched longer than cold muscles. Badminton is a sport that requires jumping, vigorous overhead swinging motions, and quick changes of direction that use explosive power. Excessive stretching and time spent warming up may actually reduce strength temporarily. Therefore many experts recommend stretching after a workout rather than before. Badminton competition would seem to emphasize a need for both aerobic and anaerobic fitness along with a warm-up exercise program. It is the individual player's choice whether to stretch before or after strenuous exercise.

Here are some basic static stretches for badminton players. Hold each stretch for 20 to 30 seconds.

• **Shoulder shrug** (figure 11.1). Begin in a standing position with your arms at your sides. Elevate and then lower your shoulders, returning to the starting position. This motion stretches and then relaxes the neck and trapezius muscles.

• **Neck stretch** (figure 11.2). From a standing position, stretch your neck laterally, bringing your ear toward your shoulder. Alternate this stretch to the right and then to the left. You may assist this stretch by alternately pushing on the side of the head with each hand. This active stretch can aid in warming up your neck muscles.

• **Triceps stretch** (figure 11.3). Begin in a standing position. Alternate stretching and warming up the triceps muscles of both arms. Alternate placing each arm behind the head and then assisting the stretch with the opposite hand and arm. As the hand reaches down the back, the opposite hand is placed on the elbow and provides slight pressure to enhance the stretch of the triceps muscle.

Figure 11.1 Shoulder shrug.

Figure 11.2 Neck stretch.

Figure 11.3 Triceps stretch.

• **Shoulder stretch** (figure 11.4). Stretch each shoulder alternately by placing the arm in a horizontal position across the chest as if reaching for an imaginary object to the left and then to the right. When reaching with the right arm across the chest, the left hand and arm are placed below the arm of the shoulder being stretched. This pulling motion assists the stretch and aids in warming up the shoulder joints and muscles.

Figure 11.4 Shoulder stretch.

• **Quadriceps stretch** (figure 11.5). Begin in a standing position. Stretch both legs by alternately positioning the leg in a flexed position behind the body. While standing on one leg, reach behind and grasp your foot. Pull your foot slightly toward your buttocks. Alternate stretching and warming up the fronts of each quadriceps or upper thighs.

• **Crossover toe touch** (figure 11.6). Begin in a standing position. Cross the right foot over the left while remaining in a standing position. Bend or flex at the waist and attempt to touch the toes of both feet. Reverse the crossover position by crossing the left foot over the right and repeat the stretch. Alternate stretching and warming up the hamstring muscles of each leg.

Figure 11.5 Quadriceps stretch.

Figure 11.6 Crossover toe touch.

• **Calf stretch** (figure 11.7). Begin in a standing position. Assume a stride position with one leg significantly in front of the other. With the rear foot remaining flat on the court surface, flex the front knee and bend forward. Reverse the position of the legs and then stretch the calf muscle of the opposite leg. Alternate the stretch and warm up the calf muscle or gastrocnemius in both lower legs.

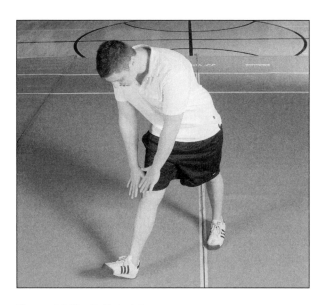

Figure 11.7 Calf stretch.

Concentration

Concentration is the ability of a player to shut out any outside or extraneous interference. Mental practice might involve reviewing game situations over and over in your mind or actually perceiving yourself executing good shots and winning games. Modern technology allows anyone to watch the very best athletes in any sport. Watching the proper technique of experts on a videotape allows you to observe the correct way to perform the strokes and serves. You may also videotape yourself and see how closely your form resembles theirs. Some studies have gone so far as to edit out all of the improper techniques and record only the strokes that were executed well. Then the subject observes himself or herself performing the stroke correctly. Some research indicates that this type of visual feedback alone, even without physical practice, can improve quality of play. Another technique involving mental imagery is to close your eyes and visualize yourself winning or playing well. Finally, relaxation seems to also improve the ability to concentrate and react more quickly during competition.

Prevention of Injuries

Common injuries in badminton are sprains, strains, fractures, and cramps. Of all the injuries to which badminton players are prone, those affecting the ankle and the foot have the greatest incidence.

A sprained ankle is a ligament injury. It results from a sudden twist or rolling over (inversion) of the foot, causing the outside (lateral) ligaments to be stretched or torn. Eighty-five percent of all ankle injuries are of this type.

Ankle fractures are caused by a sudden wrenching or twisting, the same factors that cause sprains. However, fractures usually result from excessive force outward (eversion) in relation to the leg.

A strain is a muscle or tendon injury. Landing from a jump exposes the tendons of the ankle and muscles of the foot to the danger of strain. As a badminton player lands, particularly on the overhead motion of the around-the-head shot or the smash, the nondominant foot absorbs shock three to four times the player's weight. This may give the Achilles tendon a sudden stretch beyond its normal range of motion and thus tear or strain the tendon. Strength training along with stretching and warm-up exercises are the best means of preventing this type of traumatic injury Proper footwork and footwear enhance the ability to land and change direction quickly and efficiently without causing injury. A torn Achilles tendon is a serious injury that may require surgery as well as a long rehabilitation process.

Knee injuries are another common problem for badminton players at all levels. When the knee is subjected to the extraordinary stress of running, jumping, lunging, or pivoting (any of which can involve weight loads of up to 1,000 pounds, or 454 kg), trauma to the knee is a real possibility. The cartilage or meniscus is probably the most frequently injured component of the knee. This half-moon shaped cushion acts as a shock absorber between the shin (tibia) and the thigh (femur). The old treatment for a torn meniscus was to remove it completely, which led to hospitalization, a long recovery process, and a large scar. However, with the refinement of arthroscopic surgery, a small incision is made through which only the torn part of the meniscus is removed. This allows for a much shorter rehabilitation period of only a few days instead of several months. Another frequent site of knee injury is the ligament. If any of the seven ligaments in each knee is stretched or torn, the knee becomes very unstable. Replacement of the lost ligament tissue with tendon tissue from elsewhere in the body, or with Gore-Tex (a synthetic material used to make waterproof rain gear), are potential solutions.

The elbow is also particularly susceptible to trauma or stress from repetitive overuse. The overhead throwing motion of both the forehand and the backhand generates a severe whiplash action (particularly if executed incorrectly) from which soreness can arise due to fatigue and minor strains from overload. Tennis elbow is a popular, generic term covering several ailments. In general, they are chronic conditions resulting from overuse of certain forearm muscles. They have in common tenderness about the elbow and pain upon attempting to extend the arm, rotate the forearm, or grip an object.

The solution to these common injuries suggests that prevention is the best medicine. Warming up and stretching can reduce sprains and strains to muscles and joints. A hot shower can increase body temperature, loosen you up, and possibly prevent a strain. Before playing, go through a series of basic stretches. Take a minimum of 5 minutes to stretch the ankles and Achilles tendons, the hamstrings, the quadriceps (thighs), and the back, shoulders, and arms. Do all stretches slowly with little or no bouncing. Also include in the warm-up about 5 to 10 minutes of easy hitting before starting the match.

Any injury that produces swelling should be iced until the swelling is eliminated. The use of heat or liniment should be reserved for muscle pulls or strain-type injuries as well as for muscle soreness. Massaging the tired muscles aids in preventing muscle soreness and speeds up recovery from fatigue. Research indicates that you can prevent cramps and muscle soreness by keeping your body well hydrated. Drink plenty of liquids before, during, and after heavy exercise. Some of the electrolyte solutions (Gatorade, Powerade, and All Sport, for example) seem to prevent muscle soreness if consumed before, during, and after exercise. Sugar content, temperature, and quantity all affect the speed at which liquids are absorbed by the body. High-sugared drinks (over 10 percent) are absorbed much more slowly than plain water or low-sugar drinks (6 to 8 percent). Cool water is absorbed faster than tap water or warm drinks. Larger quantities are also absorbed faster. A few swallows of water at the drinking fountain are not absorbed as fast as a large glass (16 to 20 ounces, or about half a liter) of liquid.

Weight Training

Weight training is designed to develop muscular strength and muscular endurance. In badminton, you need muscular strength and endurance to move and to execute every stroke.

Generally, the use of heavy loads with a small number of repetitions emphasizes development of muscular strength, while relatively light or moderate loads with a larger number of repetitions emphasizes muscular endurance. For the badminton player with little experience in weight training, the following plan is recommended. Select an amount of weight for each exercise that permits 10 to 12 repetitions before fatigue sets in (usually 30 to 50 pounds [13.6 to 22.7 kg] will suffice for most of the exercises listed). Lift this weight every other day, attempting to increase the number of repetitions. Repeat this cycle indefinitely. After you attain 15 repetitions

or more, add more weight until only 10 or 12 repetitions are possible again. Also, to develop and maintain flexibility, perform each exercise through a full range of motion around the joints involved. The following areas need muscular strength and muscular endurance development specific to badminton play:

- Hands and wrists
- Biceps and triceps
- Hamstrings and quadriceps
- Calf (gastrocnemius) muscles
- Abdominal muscles
- Back and shoulders
- Neck

Free weights such as dumbbells or bar bells are commonly used in weight resistance training programs. A simple exercise to develop muscular strength and endurance of the hands and wrists is to continually squeeze a rubber ball such as a racquetball or a squash ball. This can be done periodically during the day or as part of a scheduled workout. Numerous types of commercial weight-training equipment are also available. Nautilus, Universal, Keiser, Cybex, and Body Masters are only a few of the brand names that manufacture equipment that can improve muscular strength and muscular endurance through weight resistance training exercises.

Conditioning Drill 1. *Box of 50*

Place a box of 50 shuttles on a chair or a table or have a third player on one side of the court near the T area holding the box. Player A begins with 8 to 12 shuttles held in one hand. He or she throws one shuttle at a time over the net to player B. Player B may hit any return other than a clear. His or her primary objective is to get the shuttle on the floor as soon as possible. In addition, player B must try to recover to centercourt after each shot. Therefore, player A must pause slightly between throws to give player B enough time to recover. However, you can make the drill progressively more difficult by giving less and less

time between throws. This speeding of the throws forces player B to move more quickly and serves as a good means of physical conditioning. Even if player B misses or fails to reach a return, player A should continue until all 50 shuttles have been thrown. Players then rotate positions and alternate until each has completed 1 to 3 sets.

To Increase Difficulty

- Give less time between throws.

To Decrease Difficulty

- Give more time between throws.

Success Check

- Use proper footwork for efficient and fast movement.
- Use proper grip for different strokes.
- Contact shuttle as soon as possible with proper stroke execution.

Score Your Success

Complete box of 50 with 10 misses or less = 10 points

Complete box of 50 with 11 to 15 misses = 5 points

Complete box of 50 with 16 to 20 misses = 1 point

Your score ___

Conditioning Drill 2. *Forehand Clear and Backhand Drop*

Player A starts near centerline, 3 to 4 feet from the short service line, to receive the initial serve. Player B serves high to player A's deep, forehand corner (figure 11.8). Player A returns the serve with a straight-ahead clear to player B's deep, backhand corner. Player B returns this clear with a straight-ahead backhand drop shot. Player A moves into the net and returns the drop shot with an underhand clear to player B's deep, forehand corner, and they repeat the sequence.

Success Check

- Recover to your ready position after each shot.

- Hit clears high and deep.
- Let drop shots fall close to the top of the net.

Score Your Success

Continue the rally for 5 minutes or more without a miss = 10 points

Continue the rally for 3 or 4 minutes without a miss = 5 points

Continue the rally for 1 or 2 minutes without a miss = 1 point

Your score ___

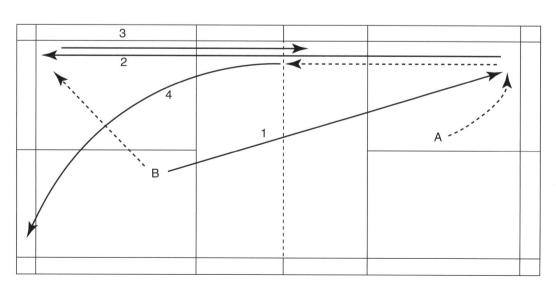

Figure 11.8 Forehand clear and backhand drop.

Conditioning Drill 3. *Three-Shot Continuous Rally*

Player A begins the rally with an underhand clear to player B's deep forehand corner (figure 11.9). Player B returns this clear with a straight-ahead drop shot or smash to player A's backhand. A smash return will carry deeper into the court. Still player A will return either shot with a straight drop shot. Player B then clears deep to player A's deep forehand corner, and they repeat the three-shot sequence: clear, drop or smash, drop.

Success Check

- Hit clears high and deep.
- Hit smashes downward with some pace.
- Let drop shots fall close to the top of the net.

Score Your Success

Complete four three-shot rallies without a miss = 10 points

Complete three three-shot rallies without a miss = 5 points

Complete two three-shot rallies without a miss = 1 point

Your score ___

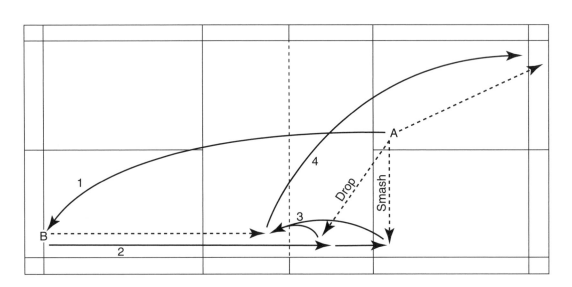

Figure 11.9 Three-shot continuous rally.

Conditioning Drill 4. *Crosscourt Three-Shot Continuous Rally*

Player A begins the rally with an underhand clear to player B's deep forehand corner (figure 11.10). Player B returns this clear with a crosscourt drop shot or smash to player A's forehand. Player A returns this net drop shot with a straight-ahead net drop shot. Player B then clears deep to player A's deep forehand corner, and they repeat the three-shot sequence: clear, drop or smash, drop.

Success Check

- Hit clears high and deep.
- Hit smashes downward with some pace.
- Let drop shots fall close to the top of the net.

172

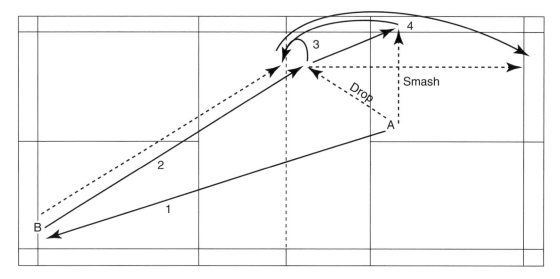

Figure 11.10 Crosscourt three-shot continuous rally.

Score Your Success

Complete four three-shot rallies without a miss = 10 points

Complete three three-shot rallies without a miss = 5 points

Complete two three-shot rallies without a miss = 1 point

Your score ___

Conditioning Drill 5. *Six-Shooter Footwork Rally*

In this three-player drill, one player (B) must cover the court quickly by moving up, back, and diagonally. This drill provides conditioning, stroke production, and footwork practice. Player

C is stationed in backcourt and begins the rally by clearing to player B's deep forehand court (figure 11.11). Player B hits a forehand overhead clear straight ahead to player C's deep backhand.

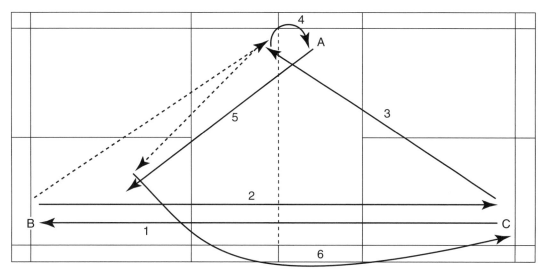

Figure 11.11 Six-shooter footwork rally.

Player C hits a crosscourt drop to player B's left frontcourt. Player B redrops with a spin or tumble net drop shot. Player A, stationed at the net, immediately hits the net drop shot with a quick, flat return to player B's deep right backcourt. Player B clears out of his or her right backcourt. This sequence forces you to move quickly, even more quickly than you would like to, in order to cover the singles court.

After five rallies, rotate clockwise. Perform the drill until each player has attempted five rallies.

Success Check

- Hit clears high and deep.
- Let drop shots tumble and fall close to the top of the net.
- Hit drive shots quickly and flat.

Score Your Success

Complete four rallies without a miss = 10 points

Complete three rallies without a miss = 5 points

Complete two rallies without a miss = 1 point

Your score ___

Conditioning Drill 6. *Speed Attack*

Player A is a setter who sends up a shot anywhere on the opposite side of the net to player B (figure 11.12). Player B responds and then charges the net. Player C is stationed near the net and tosses a short bird just over the net. Player B closes toward the net and tries to put away the bird. Player A should hit another shot as soon as player B puts away the bird at the net. The drill is continuous for 30 to 60 seconds.

To Increase Difficulty

- Increase the pace to make it more difficult for player B to recover in time to smash again.

- Vary the height of the toss at the net so player B has to hit a drive from the net instead of a smash.
- Have player B leap in toward the net as soon as he or she thinks contact is possible.

To Decrease Difficulty

- Slow the pace to give player B more time.
- Toss the bird at the net slightly higher to give player B more time to get there.

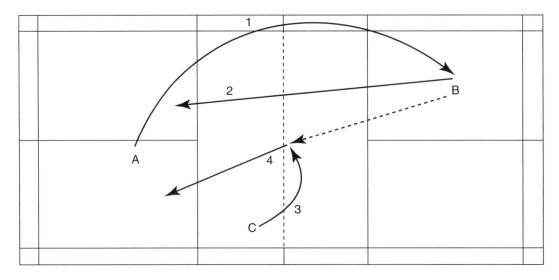

Figure 11.12 Speed attack drill.

Success Check

- Use correct footwork when moving to the net.
- Keep racket up as you near the net.

Score Your Success

Rally continuously for 30 seconds without missing = 10 points

Complete six consecutive returns without missing = 5 points

Your score ____

Conditioning Drill 7. *Deep Base Attack*

Player A stands near the back boundary line and loops an underhand shot close to the net to player B (figure 11.13). Player B straddles the back doubles service line and then charges the net as soon as the shot has been hit. Player B closes toward the net and tries to hit the bird high enough to allow him or her time to get back again. Player A should hit another shot as soon as player B recovers to the backcourt. The drill is continuous for 30 to 60 seconds.

To Increase Difficulty

- Increase the pace so player B has less time to recover to get to the net again.
- Vary the direction of the shot so player B has less time to recover from the net. Player A may increase the difficulty for player B by sending shots to the right or left, perhaps with a fake.

To Decrease Difficulty

- Slow the pace to give player B more time.
- Hit the bird at the net slightly higher to give player B more time.

Success Check

- Use correct footwork when moving to the net.
- Keep your racket up as you move and recover.

Score Your Success

Rally continuously for 60 seconds without missing = 10 points

Complete six consecutive returns without missing = 5 points

Your score ____

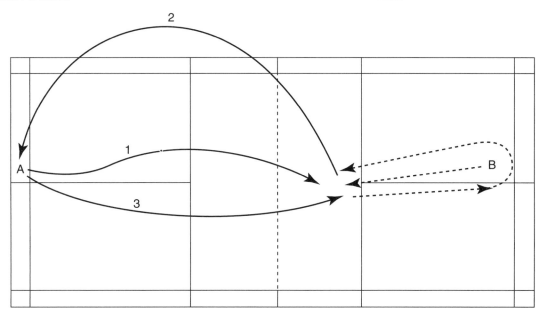

Figure 11.13   Deep base attack drill.

Conditioning Drill 8. *Footwork on Command*

This is a less advanced drill for beginners. You will need a tape recorder, another player, or a coach. In this drill, you have a set time to make each movement and return to centercourt.

The tape recorder, other player, or coach announces a preparatory command (up or back) followed by a command of execution (forehand or backhand) in a random sequence with a 1- to 2-second pause between each command. When you hear the command "up, forehand," move up to the net and swing as if hitting a forehand. When you hear "back, forehand," move back to the forehand or right back corner. The command "back, backhand" means to move back to the left or backhand corner. The command "up, backhand" means to move up to the front left or backhand corner at the net.

Start at centercourt in ready position. Touch the four corners of the court in random order as indicated, returning to center position after each touch. Pivot and reach with your dominant arm and leg and shuffle using a step–close stepping action with your feet. Crossover only on your backhand side, not your forehand side.

Follow the verbal commands and hand gestures as you move around the badminton court. Figure 11.14 shows a sample sequence of movement in eight directions:

1. Back forehand
2. Front forehand
3. Back backhand
4. Front backhand
5. Front forehand
6. Side backhand
7. Front backhand
8. Side forehand

This drill may be performed at slower speeds or half-speed in order to emphasize proper foot movement. After moving to the given area of the court, simulate a swing at an imaginary bird. After completing the simulated hit, recover to centercourt position as quickly as possible. Complete three successive repetitions.

To Increase Difficulty

- Increase the number of touches in any one sequence.
- Reduce the time interval between commands.
- Add additional commands, such as right, side and left, side movements.
- Use a sashay step instead of the normal step–close shuffle step.

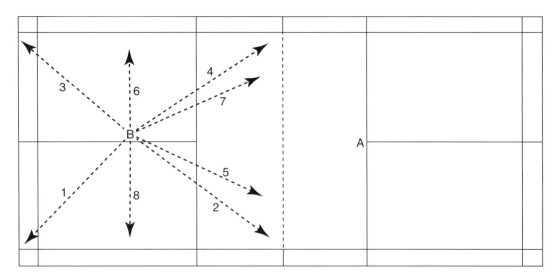

Figure 11.14 Footwork on command drill.

- Pivot, step–close jump, and simulate a stroking action at the end of the movement. Return to centercourt. This jumping action requires much more energy, and you should attempt to stay under control and on balance, especially when landing from the jump.

To Decrease Difficulty

- Decrease the number of touches in any one sequence.
- Slow down. Walk or shuffle your feet more slowly.
- The coach uses hand signals to further illustrate the direction of movement.

Success Check

- Without a racket in your hand, reach and touch the floor with your dominant hand.
- Lead with your dominant foot.
- Simulate swinging at and hitting an imaginary bird at the end of each touch or reach.

Score Your Success

Touch the four corners 10 times or more in 30 seconds = 10 points

Touch the four corners 6 to 9 times in 30 seconds = 5 points

Touch the four corners 1 to 5 times in 30 seconds = 1 point

Your score ____

Conditioning Drill 9. *By the Numbers*

This is a more advanced drill. You will need a tape recorder or a metronome. You will have a set time for each movement and return to centercourt. The tape recorder announces a number in a random sequence with a 1- to 2-second pause between each number. Each number corresponds to a position on the court:

- Number 1 indicates up to the net or forehand.
- Number 2 indicates back to the forehand or right back corner.
- Number 3 indicates back to the left or backhand corner.
- Number 4 indicates up to the front left or backhand corner at the net.

A sample sequence is 1, 4, 2, 4, 2, 2, 1, 4, 3, 4, 2, 1, 2, 2, 4.

Start at centercourt in ready position. Touch the four corners of the court in random order as commanded by the tape recorded message, returning to the center position after each touch. Emphasize proper footwork and speed of movement. Perform this drill at normal or full-speed.

Pivot and reach with your dominant arm and leg and shuffle using a step–close stepping action with your feet. Crossover only on your backhand side, not your forehand side. Perform the drill for as many numbers are called.

To Increase Difficulty

- Reduce the time interval between each number announced.
- Simulate swinging at and hitting an imaginary bird at the end of each touch or reach.
- Use a sashay step instead of the normal step–close shuffle step.
- Pivot, step–close jump, and simulate a stroking action at the end. Return to centercourt. This jumping action requires much more energy, and you should attempt to stay under control and on balance, especially when landing from the jump.

To Decrease Difficulty

- Slow down or increase the time interval between numbers called. Walk or shuffle your feet more slowly.

Success Check

- Without a racket in your hand, reach and touch the floor with your dominant hand.
- Lead with your dominant foot.

MOVEMENT AND REACTION

The rally scoring system forces players to focus on consistency. It is imperative to play as error free as possible. The objective is to increase the quality of the shot delivered. Advanced players should work for consistency while maintaining a high quality of execution and shot selection.

During drills, the feeder controls the speed and the flight path of shuttles. The pace will increase or decrease the amount of time that the player has to react. It is critical that players walk away with a sense of accomplishment. The feeder should maintain a level that allows the player to keep the rally going and not try to hit impossible shots to the player. Advanced players must learn how to sustain a rally. The feeder must push and slow down as necessary so that the player will develop stamina and consistency. The coach or instructor should provide feedback and positive reinforcement, making sure the player knows the difference between gliding through the drill and pushing at 100 percent. The player must return to center after all return drops. This replicates game situations and increases the player's ability to recognize the speed of game situations. It will also work on change of direction and recovery after the shot. In observing changes of direction, the coach or instructor should look for proper weight transfer and activation speed. This will indicate the player's state of conditioning. Endurance is important because when the athlete is fatigued, his or her consistency will decline or may disappear altogether.

The following conditioning drills are presented in a circuit training format. These 11 drills are performed for 5 minutes each and then players rotate to the next station. They emphasize agility, reaction, speed, and power.

1. **Drive and push drill inside small rectangle.** Two players of equal skill drive the shuttle back and forth, with a random push shot directed behind the other's shoulders. Players keep score and use half-court. Players are allowed to hit the shuttle between the short service line and doubles long service line only. Execute the drill for 5 minutes. This station encourages each player should continually change tactics and attempt to find areas or shots to knock opponents off balance.

2. **Endurance and strength.** Player A begins in left service court. He or she hits a high, deep clear, trying to stay within 10 inches (0.25 m) inside of the singles side line. Player B cross clears to the opposite corner, working on strength to get a deep and solid shot. As they get better, they can hit offensive clears occasionally. Players switch roles after 2 minutes.

3. **Defensive and offensive drills.** (1) Player A smashes to either side, and player B lifts back. Players switch roles after 2 minutes. Repeat drill. (2) Player A straight drives and player B cross drives. Players switch roles after 2 minutes. Repeat drill. (3) Player A straight drops, and player B cross drops. Players switch roles after 2 minutes. Repeat drill.

4. **Explosive movement.** For drops, the feeder feeds shuttles to the player. The player straight drops 50 shuttles per side and cross drops 50 shuttles per side. Hand toss to start. Toss deep to work tighter toward the net. For impossible drops, the feeder feeds shuttles to

the player but the player stands farther back than usual. The player arrives at the drop at a less-than-optimal height and position. This drill works on extension and flexibility. After 2 minutes, switch roles and repeat drill.

A continuation of the explosive movement drill requires the player to shadow a net shot, taking one step back toward the center. The feeder then hits a quick shot to the rear, forcing the player to move explosively while maintaining balance. The choice of the shot contributes to the ease of recovery. Repeat to at least two corners. The player makes quick changes of direction with explosive movement and considerable agility. After 1 minute, switch roles and repeat drill.

5. **Drop and clear.** Player A stands at the right corner of the net. Player B stands at the left corner of backcourt. Player C (worker) hits to both for consistency. Player A drops straight and player B clears straight. After several rallies, player B varies shots, clearing straight and crossing and dropping straight or crossing. Later player B drops straight or crosscourt.

6. **Change-of-direction shuttle run.** Start with 12 shuttles, 6 shuttles at front and 3 on each mid court sideline. Player must lunge and change directions, attempting to knock down each of the shuttles.

7. **Two-on-one defense.** Two players hit to one player for 5 minutes. Hit smashes, drops, and offensive clears. The two players assume front and back positions.

8. **Two-on-one offense.** The solo player smashes, drops, and performs offensive clears. Two players defend. The two players are side by side.

9. **Three-on-one defense.** Two players in front and one in back. The solo player defends.

10. **Side smash with cross return.** The first shot demands consistency; the second shot works on recovery and reaction to the returning shot. Work on control of the shot after a demand is put on your body. The smash can be made from both sides of the court with crosscourt returns. You can increase the difficulty by changing from flat drive returns to high clear returns.

11. **Side around-the-head with cross return.** This drill works on recovery after executing an around-the-head shot, which taxes the body and incorporates a rapid weight transfer and change of direction. Player executes around-the-head smash, partner returns crosscourt. The player must retrieve the crosscourt shot and execute a drive return down the same line. The player's goal is to hit 10 in a row three times. Five trials allowed maximum. Perform the drill to both corners of the net.

SUCCESS SUMMARY OF CONDITIONING

A structured badminton conditioning program varies depending on the player's current physical fitness, ability, and skill level. Any badminton player can become a better player by being more physically fit. Muscular strength and muscular endurance are important factors in overall fitness. They also aid in improving speed, agility, and power on the badminton court.

Conditioning Drills

1. Box of 50	___ out of 10
2. Forehand Clear and Backhand Drop	___ out of 10
3. Three-Shot Continuous Rally	___ out of 10
4. Crosscourt Three-Shot Continuous Rally	___ out of 10
5. Six-Shooter Footwork Rally	___ out of 10
6. Speed Attack	___ out of 10
7. Deep Base Attack	___ out of 10
8. Footwork on Command	___ out of 10
9. By the Numbers	___ out of 10
Total	**___ out of 90**

If you scored at least 75 out of a possible 90 points, you have sufficiently mastered this step. If you scored fewer than 75 points, repeat the drills that were difficult for you. Have a coach, instructor, or experienced player evaluate your skill.

You have completed the step-by-step process to learn the sport of badminton. *Badminton: Steps to Success, Second Edition,* follows a learning sequence developed over a long playing and teaching career. Each step prepares you for the next one and moves you closer to becoming the best badminton player you can be. The emphasis on fundamentals and strategy allows you to analyze what you are doing on the badminton court. Suggestions to increase or decrease the difficulty of the drills allows you to pace your progress to match your ability. Missteps identify typical problems experienced by players learning badminton and provide suggestions for correcting those problems.

Congratulations on reaching the top of the *Badminton: Steps to Success* staircase. Continue to read, ask questions, observe, and imitate more experienced players, and, most of all, practice and play badminton. *Badminton: Steps to Success, Second Edition,* presents the formula for success in badminton. The only other elements you need to add are your talent, desire, and personality.

◪ Glossary

alley—The playing area that comes into or out of play at various times during any game. For example, the side alley is the playing area on each side of the court between the singles sideline and the doubles sideline. This 1.5-foot (0.46 m) wide area is in play for doubles, but out of bounds for singles. The back alley is an area 2.5 feet (0.76 m) deep between the doubles back service line and the back boundary line. It is out of bounds on any doubles serve. After the serve is in play, this alley is in bounds for any other return.

around-the-head stroke—A return made with a forehand stroke but contacted over the player's nondominant shoulder.

back boundary line—The line similar to the baseline in tennis that designates the end or back of the badminton playing area.

backcourt—Approximately the last 11 feet (3.35 m) of the court on either side of the net or midcourt to the back boundary line.

backhand—Any return or stroke hit on the nondominant side of the body.

backhand grip—The manner in which a player grasps the racket to hit any return from his or her nondominant side. In badminton, this is usually done with the handshake, or pistol, grip, held with the dominant thumb in an up position on the top left bevel of the handle.

backswing—That part of the swing that takes the racket back in preparation for the forward swing.

Badminton World Federation—The governing body for badminton play and competition throughout the world. Formerly the International Badminton Federation or IBF; the name change was effective December 2006.

base—A spot near the middle of the court that a player tries to return to after most shots.

baseline—The line designating the back boundary of the court.

bird—The missile or object struck with the badminton racket that begins the rally over the net. Same as shuttle or shuttlecock.

carry—A return that is caught on the racket face and is slung or thrown over the net. It is sometimes referred to as a sling or a throw. This is a legal return as long as it is a continuation of the player's normal stroke and is not a double hit.

clear—A high return that carries deep into the backcourt.

crosscourt—A return or stroke that sends the bird diagonally across the court.

double hit—A fault that occurs when the shuttle is hit twice in succession on the same stroke.

doubles service court—The serving area into which the doubles serve must be delivered. Each side of a badminton court has a right and a left service court for doubles. Each doubles service court is bounded by the short service line, the centerline, the doubles sideline, and the doubles back service line. Its dimensions are 13 feet (3.96 m) long by 10 feet (3.05 m) wide. It is sometimes referred to as short and fat. The side alley is in bounds; the back alley is not.

drive—A return or stroke that sends the shuttle in a relatively flat trajectory, parallel to the floor, but high enough to pass over the net.

drive serve—A hard, fast serve that crosses the net with a flat trajectory and is usually directed toward the receiver's nondominant shoulder. It is used more in doubles than in singles.

drop shot—A return or stroke that barely clears the net and falls toward the floor, hit underhand or overhand from the net or the backcourt.

fault—Any violation of the rules.

flick serve or flick return—An especially quick, flat serve or return initiated by a flick of the wrist that loops the bird high out of reach toward the rear of the opponent's court. It is used primarily in doubles if the opponent is consistently rushing the player's serve.

follow-through—The smooth continuation of a stroke after the racket has contacted the bird.

forehand—Any return or stroke hit on the dominant side of the body.

forehand grip—The manner in which the player grasps the racket to hit any return from his or her dominant side. The handshake, or pistol, grip is the most common forehand grip in badminton.

frontcourt—Approximately the front 11 feet (3.35 m) of the court on either side of the net or midcourt to the net. The front part of the court, sometimes referred to as the forecourt.

game—A competition that has a goal of a specified number of points. All games, such as women's or men's singles, men's and women's doubles, and mixed doubles, are played to 21 points.

hairpin drop shot—A form of drop shot played from near the net that travels up one side of the net and down the other side, thus forming a trajectory in the shape of a hairpin.

hands down—Under the rally point scoring system, in which only one partner has the opportunity to serve in any one service turn, this term no longer applies. Under the former rules, hands down was used to indicate when a doubles partner lost his or her turn to serve. One hand down meant that one partner lost his or her serve. Two hands down meant both partners had lost their serves, indicating their service turn was over and their side was out.

inning—An individual's or team's turn at serving or the serving turn on one end of the court.

International Badminton Federation—The IBF was formerly the governing body for badminton play and competition throughout the world. See *Badminton World Federation*.

let—A form of interference in which the point is replayed.

love—In scoring, meaning zero or no points have been scored.

love-all—Zero-all or no points have been scored by either side.

match—A competition that has a specified number of games. To win a match, a player usually has to win two out of three games.

match point—The point that wins the match.

mixed doubles—A four-handed game in which male and female partners team together to play on opposite sides of the net from each other.

net shot—Any return that strikes the net and continues over into the opponent's court. This might also apply to any drop shot return played from a point near the net.

overhead—Any stroke played from a point above head height.

placement—A return hit to a specific spot in the opponent's court where it will be difficult for the opponent to return.

push shot—A return or shot hit or pushed softly down into the opponent's court. In doubles, this usually means past the opposing partner stationed at the net.

rally—Any exchange back and forth across the net between opposing players during any particular point.

ready position—The basic waiting position near center-court, which is equidistant from all corners. This position affords the player the best opportunity to get to any possible return made by the opponent.

receiver—Any player who receives the serve.

return—Any method of hitting an opponent's shots back over the net.

serve or service—The act of putting the shuttle into play at the beginning of a point or rally.

server—The player who delivers the serve.

service court—One of the two half-courts divided by the net into which the serve must be directed. There are right and left service courts for singles and doubles play. They differ in size and shape.

service over—Loss of serve, serve goes over to the opponent.

short service line—The front line designating the beginning of the service court and situated 6 feet 6 inches (1.98m) from the net.

shuttle or shuttlecock—The missile used in badminton. Same as bird.

side out—Loss of service. Same as service over or hands down in doubles play.

singles service court—The serving area into which the singles serve must be delivered. Each side of a badminton court has a right and a left service court for singles. Each singles service court is bounded by the short service line, the centerline, the singles sideline and the back boundary line. Its dimensions are 15.5 feet (5.03 m) long by 8.5 feet (2.59 m) wide. It is sometimes referred to as long and narrow.

singles sideline—The singles sideline designates the out-of-bounds for singles play. The singles court is 17 feet wide (5.18 m) from sideline to sideline.

smash—A powerful overhead return or stroke hit at a downward angle into the opponent's court with excessive speed.

stroke—The act of hitting the bird with the racket.

Thomas Cup—A men's international badminton team competition similar to the Davis Cup in tennis. It was first held in 1948. Six singles and three doubles matches are played between two countries. Thomas Cup competition is held on a two-year cycle in the even years.

Uber Cup—A women's international team competition. It began in 1957 and was named for a former English player, Mrs. H.S. Uber. It is also held on a two-year cycle in the even years.

USA Badminton—USA Badminton is the national governing body for badminton in the United States. USA Badminton was the American Badminton Association from 1936 until 1977, when it was reorganized and renamed the United States Badminton Association. In 1996, the current name, USA Badminton, was adopted for membership purposes.

wood shot—This return or shot results from the tip or cork of the shuttle hitting on the frame of the racket rather than on the strings. Although it has not always been a legal return, the IBF ruled in 1963 that wood shots were acceptable.

◰ Additional Resources

BOOKS

Ballou, R.B. 1992. *Badminton for beginners.* Englewood, CO: Morton.

Bloss, M.V., and R.S. Hales. 1990. *Badminton.* 6th ed. Dubuque, IA: Brown.

Grice, T. 2007. *Badminton.* 6th ed. Boston, American Press.

Lo, D., and K. Stark. 1991. The badminton overhead shot. *National Strength and Conditioning Association Journal.* 13, 4: 6-13, 87-89.

Schoppe, D. 1997. *Badminton for physical education and beyond.* Manhattan Beach, CA: HL Corp.

Sweeting, R.L., and J.S. Wilson. 1992. *Badminton: Basic skills and drills.* Mountain View, CA: Mayfield.

Wadood, T., and K. Tan. 1990. *Badminton today.* St. Paul: West.

EQUIPMENT SUPPLIERS

The cost and quality of badminton equipment varies greatly. The following are the two premier badminton supply companies in the United States:

Louisville Badminton Supply
1313 Lyndon Lane, Suite 103
Louisville, KY 40222
502-426-3219
www.angelfire.com/biz/lbs/index.html

San Diego Badminton Supply
2571 S. Coast Highway 101
Cardiff by the Sea, CA 92007
760-633-1996 or 1-888-badminton
www.badminton.net

Also, several internationally known companies market badminton rackets and equipment. Yonex, Carlton, and Wilson are leading manufacturers of badminton equipment worldwide.

◪ About the Author

Tony Grice has played and coached badminton for over 40 years. He has been ranked nationally as high as 11th in open men's doubles and 15th in open men's singles. At the masters level, he won the 1998 U.S. National Championship in masters men's singles, as well as the 1998 and 1999 U.S. National Championship in masters men's doubles. At the 2003 National Senior Games, he finished second in 55 + badminton singles and doubles.

Grice served as the head women's varsity badminton coach at Northwestern State University of Louisiana from 1973-1975. In 1975, two team members were among the first eight women to receive college athletic scholarships in the state of Louisiana. In 1987, Grice traveled to the World Badminton Championships in Beijing, China, as a U.S. national coach and team trainer. In addition, he was the team exercise physiologist for 10 years (1988-1999), which involved supervising several research studies at the U.S. Olympic Training Center in Colorado Springs. Grice served on the USA Badminton board of directors from 1987 to 1993. He was the coach for the South team at the 1989 Olympic Sports Festival in Oklahoma City and was an umpire at the United States Olympic Festivals in 1993 and 1995. Since 1998, Grice has served as chair of the NCAA committee for USA Badminton. He is a member of the U.S. Badminton Education Foundation and a life member of both USA Badminton and the Southern Badminton Association.

Grice is currently an associate professor in kinesiology and health science at Louisiana State University in Shreveport (LSUS). He is the author of two badminton textbooks, one of which has been published in six languages. He continues to teach badminton at LSUS.